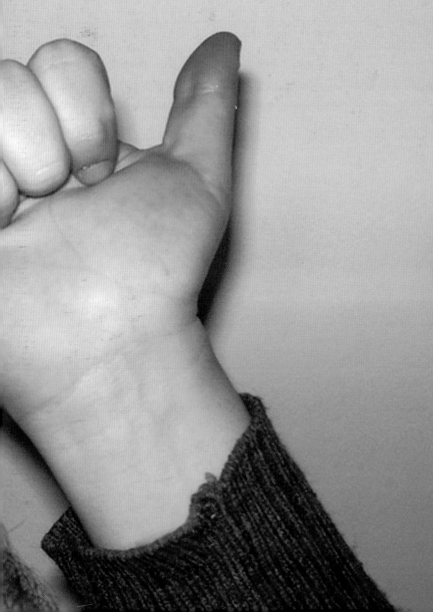

48°12`0``
North
16°22`0``
East

Publishing by
INDEX BOOK, SL
Consell de Cent 160 Local 3
08015 Barcelona
phone +34 93 454 55 47
fax +34 93 454 84 38
email: ib@indexbook.com
www.indexbook.com

About the Book
All contents are selected by
Juland Barcelona Vienna
Author and Art direction Andrés Fredes
www.julandscape.com
andres.fredes@julandscape.com

For any questions about the
Around Europe edition:
everything@aroundeuropeonline.com

ISBN 978-84-92643-76-9
Printed in China

About:

EXPE
RIMENTAL
UNCON
VENTIONAL
INNO
VATIVE
EU
ROPEAN
PACKA
GING
.

Around Europe Packaging

Another way of travelling around Europe

PACKAGING CREATES THE MOOD OF THE PRODUCT.

Around Europe Packaging, provides all the elements to become a graphic book for the lovers of quality design and a big help to all those who are searching for inspiration in creative design packaging.

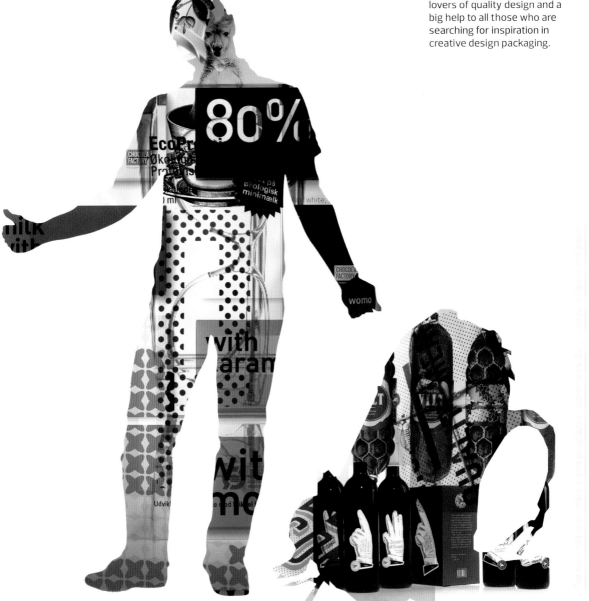

On this tour we will drift hitchhiking
across various European countries as
usual, but this time we have included
even a few more which also are in
Europe. Welcome all!

Austria
Belgium
Denmark
Cyprus
France
Germany
Greece
Iceland
Ireland
Norway
Portugal
Spain
Sweden
Switzerland
The Netherlands
United Kingdom
Best of the East:
    Czech Republic
    Romania
    Russia
    Serbia
    Slovakia
    Turkey
    Ukraine

WHAT IS PACKAGING?
It's the science, art and technology of
enclosing and protecting products.

FUNCTIONAL REQUIREMENTS:
It has to contain, wrap, identify, describe,
protect, display, promote, make it market–
able, keep it clean, attract attention,
increase density, storage, sale, distribution,
use, shipping, deliver, present, be easy to
carry, easy to store, non breakable, prevent
spoiling, tampering, breakage, and theft.
Packaging also informs the user about
product uses and benefits, product type,
quantity, number+size of servings.

SALES REQUIREMENTS:
Durability, size, opening, recyclability,
labeling, attention drawing power, quality,
branding, displaying important information.
PACKAGING CREATES
THE MOOD OF THE PRODUCT.
Consumer Packaging: contain + communicate
Used materials are very important, they
give the feeling of a product.
Sometimes packaging is part of the product.
Packaging has a PHYSICAL and
a PSYCHOLOGICAL function.

Welcome friends to another edition of Around Europe. This time, we are into Packaging. As it is already common in this book series, we will visit different European countries looking for the most interesting work of studios standing out by their quality output. Although Around Europe Packaging does not seek to be an encyclopaedia of design, it provides all the elements to become a graphic book for the lovers of quality design and a big help to all those who are searching for inspiration in creative design packaging.

In previous books of this series we toured the underground train stations of several European cities, we were on a journey boarding different airlines to enjoy the gradually vanishing airline meals of the different passenger classes. The last book contained strange post and postcards from all around Europe. In this volume we plan a journey with our personal packaging ... our suitcase or backpack. We'll travel the European roads, visiting a big amount of studios and hitchhiking to get to our favourite destinations. Be prepared. The trip is starting right NOW!

Enjoy this long design trip and be all smiles to be taken along to the best studios all around Europe.

Now it is time for acknowledgement.

I'd like to thank our collaborators. All the participants in the book come first ... You will find all their names in the index. The good vibes among all of them deserve my most sincere gratitude. You all are great professionals and, of course, I hope to have you around in future publications ... THANKS.
Also thanks to:
Marie Boltenstern, for her collaboration in this publication, for her design and coordination work.
Stefan, for his help and proof reading.
Julia, for her commitment and support.
Mia Filipa, for her smile and her love.
Titus León, for his interest and love to me.
My mother, for her love.
To Sylvie, Neus and Toni, for remembering me all christmas and because you make me happy with the good mood you have.
To Isabel, Elvira and the team of Indexbook, for their constant support and interest in our work. You are a great team.
To the photographers for their immediate interest in participating in this book.
Please find all contacts in the index.

To all thank you very much!

Enjoy the book.
visit www.indexbook.com
And be ready for a further title of Around Europe soon.
Always check
www.aroundeuropeonline.com

NEVER A FINGER WAS SO IMPORTANT
AS IN THIS TRIP... YOU WILL SEE!

AUSTRIA

47°20´ NORTH / 13°20´ WEST

AT

country
AUSTRIA

CITY   **PROJECT**
vienna   *dreh&drink*
STUDIO   **DESIGNER**
buero x   *andreas*
        miedaner
        CLIENT
        maresi
        austria ag

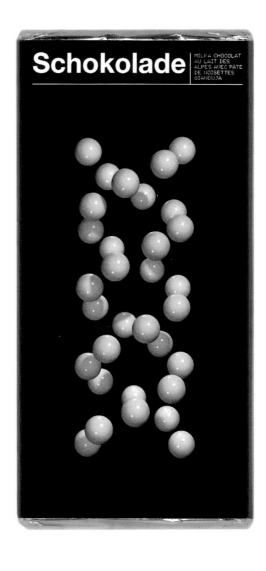

PROJECT
schafft:wissen
water/chocolate
DESIGNER
andreas miedaner
günter eder
CLIENT
akademie der
wissenschaften
austria

PROJECT
bob
mobile phone
DESIGNER
andreas miedaner
werner singer
CLIENT
mobilkom
austria ag

country
AUSTRIA

CITY   **PROJECT**
linz   *landgarten*
STUDIO *sweetie fruit*
d.signwerk **DESIGNER**
           peter schmid
           daniela waser
           CLIENT
           landgarten

PROJECT
lembach pur
fruit juices
DESIGNER
peter schmid
andrea grasser
CLIENT
lembach pur

Apfel:
Cassis

Eine geheime Sommerliebe auf
einer dunkelroten Gartenbank

Birne:
Williams naturtrüb

Sehnsüchtige Blicke
beim Vorübergehen am Gartenzaun

Apfel:
Waldbeere

Heimlicher Kuss des Waldes
im funkelnden Sommerlicht

Apfel·Karotte
Stürmisches Herzklopfen,
mittags belauscht im Gemüsegarten

Apfel·Holunder
Verhängnisvolle Liaison
mit einer holden, geistreichen Dame

PROJECT
bioemsan
cosmetics
DESIGNER
peter schmid
andrea grasser
CLIENT
multikraft

PROJECT
fandler oils
DESIGNER
peter schmid
bianca olbrich
CLIENT
ölmühle fandler

RAUBEN
KERNŒL
DT

gepresst, 100% naturrein

WALNUSS
ŒL

kaltgepresst, 100% naturrein

LEINŒL

kaltgepresst, 100% naturrein,
wöchentlich frisch gepresst.

MACADAMIA
NUSSŒL

kaltgepresst, 100% naturrein

HANFŒL

kaltgepresst, 100% naturrein

BIO-
LEINOL

kaltgepresst | 100% naturrein
wöchentlich frisch gepresst

BIO-
DISTELOL

kaltgepresst | 100% naturrein

PROJECT
fandler vinegars
DESIGNER
peter schmid
elisabeth
weggemann
CLIENT
ölmühle fandler

BIO-
APFELESSIG

im Eichenfass gereift

BIO-
WEISSWEIN-
ESSIG

aus Grünem Veltliner

BIO-
ROTWEIN-
ESSIG

aus Blauem Zweigelt

LASS DIE SONNE
SCHEINEN
GENIESSE DIE WOHLTUENDE WIRKUNG
WÄRMENDEN INGWERS MIT DIESER
FEINSTEN BIOLOGISCHEN
TEEMISCHUNG

MAGIE DES
LEBENS
ENTDECKE DAS GEHEIMNIS KOSTBAREN
WEISSEN TEES MIT DIESER FEINSTEN
BIOLOGISCHEN TEEMISCHUNG

ENERGIE IST
ÜBERALL
SPÜRE DIE STILLE KRAFT DES SANFTEN
GRÜNTEES MIT DIESER FEINSTEN
BIOLOGISCHEN TEEMISCHUNG

BASIS DEINER
SEELE
FINDE LIEBEVOLLEN AUSGLEICH IN DIESER
FEINSTEN BIOLOGISCHEN
TEEMISCHUNG MIT ERLESENEN
KRÄUTERN

INSPIRATION
DER SINNE
BELEBE DEINE WAHRNEHMUNG DURCH
SCHWARZEN TEE MIT EDLEN
GEWÜRZEN IN DIESER FEINSTEN
BIOLOGISCHEN TEEMISCHUNG

SÜSSE MOMENTE
FEIERN
KRÖNE BESONDERE AUGENBLICKE MIT
DIESER FEINSTEN BIOLOGISCHEN
TEEMISCHUNG MIT AUSGEWÄHLTEN
FRÜCHTEN

PROJECT
sonnentor
tea pyramids
DESIGNER
peter schmid
bianca olbrich
CLIENT
sonnentor

PROJECT
besser bio fruit or
natural yogurts
DESIGNER
peter schmid
andrea grasser
CLIENT
bio molkerei
lembach

PROJECT
besser bio
whey drinks
DESIGNER
peter schmid
karin bernecker
CLIENT
bio molkerei
lembach

PROJECT
alex buch
neuheitenkatalog
DESIGNER
peter schmid
daniela waser
CLIENT
alex – eine
buchhandlung

PROJECT
sonnentor
"wieder gut!" tees
DESIGNER
peter schmid
elisabeth
weggemann
CLIENT
sonnentor

PROJECT
sonnentor
schokoladen
DESIGNER
peter schmid
andrea grasser
CLIENT
sonnentor

PROJECT
d.signwerk
marmeladen
DESIGNER
peter schmid
CLIENT
d.signwerk

PROJECT
sonnentor grissinis
DESIGNER
peter schmid daniela waser
CLIENT
sonnentor

PROJECT
bioagrepa sugar
DESIGNER
peter schmid elisabeth weggemann
CLIENT
multikraft

PROJECT
sonnentor cookies
DESIGNER
peter schmid
andrea grasser
CLIENT
sonnentor

country
AUSTRIA

CITY
vienna

STUDIO
bauer –
konzept &
gestaltung

PROJECT
packaging design
wine estate türk

DESIGNER
bauer – konzept &
gestaltung

CLIENT
weingut türk

PROJECT
packaging design for wien museum
DESIGNER
bauer – konzept & gestaltung
CLIENT
wien museum

I MUSS IM FRÜH'REN LEBEN A
BLAUS G'WESEN SEIN, SONST
R' DIE SEHNSUCHT NICHT SO
SS NACH EINEM WEIN; DRUM
DEN WEIN ICH AUCH NICHT
KEN, SONDERN BEISSEN, UND
B DEN ROTEN GRAD SO GERN
S WIE DEN WEISSEN. UND
HWÖREN KÖNNT' ICH, DASS ICH
E REBLAUS G'WESEN BIN.
K: KARL FÖDERL, TEXT: ERNST MARISCHKA
NGEN VON HANS MOSER

ER SATZ CLASSIC

WIEN MUSEUM

ICH WEISS NICHT, WAS DAS IST, ICH
TRINK' SO GERN EIN GLASERL WEIN,
ES MUSS GAR KEIN BESONDERER
ANLASS UND KEIN SONNTAG SEIN,
ICH SITZ' OFT STUNDENLANG
ALLEIN AUF EINEM FLECKERL,
IN EINEM WEINLOKAL IN EINEM
STILLEN ECKERL. AN ANDEREN
MENSCHEN WÄRE DAS VIELLEICHT
ZU DUMM, DOCH ICH BIN SELIG
DORT UND WEISS GENAU, WARUM.
MUSIK: KARL FÖDERL, TEXT: ERNST MARISCHKA
GESUNGEN VON HANS MOSER

PINOT NOIR BEL

WIEN MUSEUM

PROJECT
*packaging design
for wine estate
walter fidesser*
DESIGNER
*erwin k. Bauer
birgit groismaier*
CLIENT
*ing. walter &
gertrude fidesser*

WEINVIERTEL DAC 2006 – Ried Wiege [Der Klassiker
aus dem Weinviertel]
Ein kräftiger Wein mit würzig pfeffriger Nase.
Fruchtbetont jugendlich und würzig mit gepflegtem
delikaten Säurebogen. Ein klassischer Grüner Veltliner.
Biowein aus organischem Anbau. www.fidesserwein.at

biologisch. [griech.: bios = Leben, lógos = Vernunft]
Weinbau im Einklang mit der Natur ist unser Grundsatz.
Nach den Kriterien der biologischen Landwirtschaft keltern wir
Rot- und Weißweine höchster Qualität. www.fidesserwein.at

PROJECT
*packaging design for
wine estate thallern*
DESIGNER
*erwin k. bauer
hans renzler*
CLIENT
*stiftsweingut
heiligenkreuz
freigut thallern
wein gmbh&co kg*

country
AUSTRIA

CITY   PROJECT
vienna   "stolen rags"
STUDIO   DESIGNER
katarina   katarina
soskic   soskic
    CLIENT
    self initiated

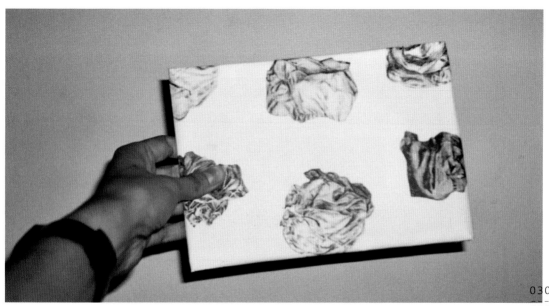

country
AUSTRIA

CITY **PROJECT**
gratwein jewelry
STUDIO packaging klotz
kopfloch **DESIGNER**
  gerlinde gruber
CLIENT
self initiated

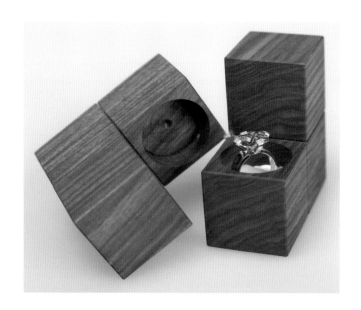

PROJECT
das ohrenprinzip
DESIGNER
gerlinde gruber
CLIENT
self initiated

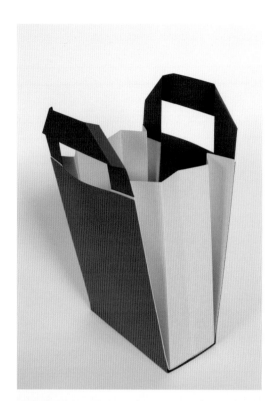

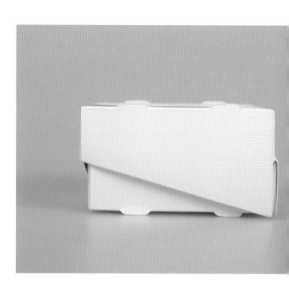

PROJECT
shopping bag rudi
DESIGNER
gerlinde gruber
CLIENT
self initiated

PROJECT
resche resi
DESIGNER
gerlinde gruber
CLIENT
self initiated

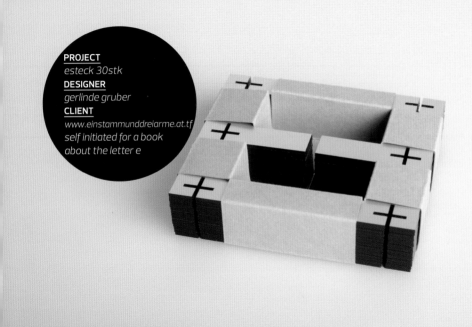

PROJECT
esteck 30stk
DESIGNER
gerlinde gruber
CLIENT
www.einstammunddreiarme.at.tf
self initiated for a book
about the letter e

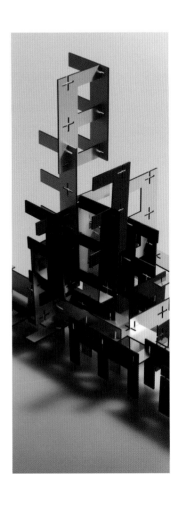

country
AUSTRIA

CITY **PROJECT**
vienna *energy bar*
STUDIO *packaging*
sl design **DESIGNER**
susanne
lippitsch
CLIENT
christian
lugar

PROJECT
paperplate
"skywalker"
DESIGNER
susanne lippitsch
CLIENT
self initiated

BELGIUM

50°50` NORTH / 4°00` EAST

BE

country
BELGIUM

CITY **PROJECT**
brussels *passanha*
STUDIO *portuguese olive oil*
base **DESIGNER**
base&photographer
michael young
CLIENT
herdeiros
passanha

PROJECT
*brand identity for
graanmarkt 13, gallery
fashion store&restaurant*
DESIGNER
base design
CLIENT
graanmarkt 13

PROJECT
*brand identity for
graanmarkt 13, gallery
fashion store&restaurant*
DESIGNER
base design
CLIENT
graanmarkt 13

CYPRUS

35°10` NORTH / 32°25` EAST

CY

country
CYPRUS

CITY **PROJECT**
paphos *diva maya*
STUDIO *tequila*
alpha **DESIGNER**
anastasia gerali
CLIENT
miravelle
distillery
mexico

me initial sketches and exploration for
EDGE product range packaging.

PROJECT
edge hair care
DESIGNER
anastasia gerali
CLIENT
*proposal for
edge hair salon
for own brand
product range*

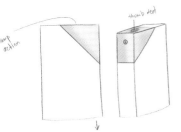

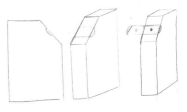

PROJECT
cowgum
electronics
DESIGNER
anastasia gerali
CLIENT
concept for off
price electronics
store

PROJECT
botanics skin care
DESIGNER
anastasia gerali
CLIENT
self initiated

DENMARK

56°00` NORTH / 10°00` EAST

DK

country
DENMARK

CITY **PROJECT**
copenhagen tracks
STUDIO headphones
aiaiai **DESIGNER**
aiaiai
CLIENT
aiaiai

Tracks Headphone w/ mic
Blue/Yellow

PROJECT
a-stand
DESIGNER
aiaiai
CLIENT
aiaiai

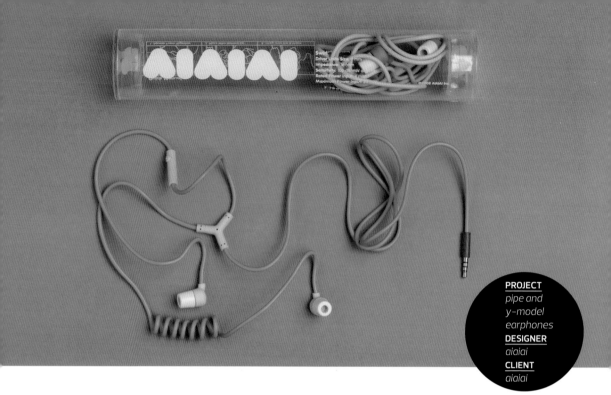

PROJECT
*pipe and
y-model
earphones*
DESIGNER
aiaiai
CLIENT
aiaiai

PROJECT
*tma – 1
headphones*
DESIGNER
aiaiai
CLIENT
aiaiai

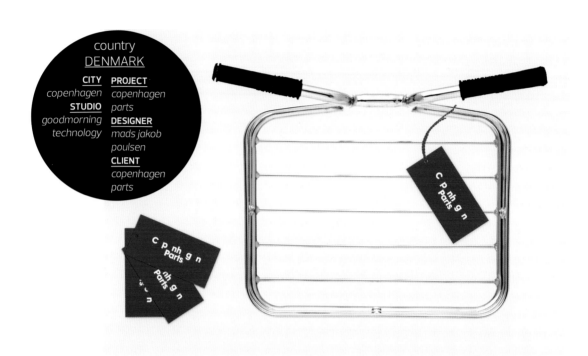

country
DENMARK

CITY **PROJECT**
copenhagen copenhagen
STUDIO parts
goodmorning **DESIGNER**
technology mads jakob
poulsen
CLIENT
copenhagen
parts

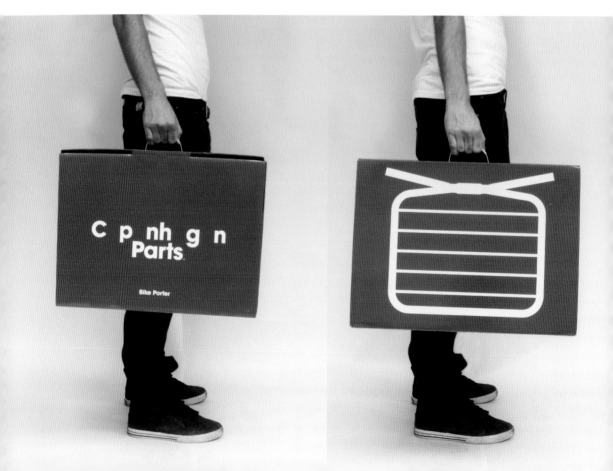

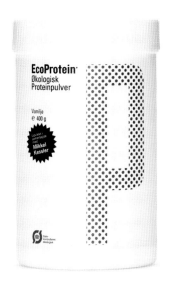

country
DENMARK

CITY **PROJECT**
copenhagen eco protein
STUDIO **DESIGNER**
mads mads
jakob jakob
poulsen poulsen
CLIENT
eco protein

3 exciting, delicious & happy condoms.

CENTER FOR
Sex & Sundhed
www.sexogsundhed.dk

3 exciting, delicious & hap

PROJECT
ribe micro
brewery
DESIGNER
mads jakob poulsen
CLIENT
ribe brewery

SEX ☺

ms.

CENTER FOR
Sex & Sundhed
www.sexogsundhed.dk

NO ☹   MORE ☺   SEX ☺

3 exciting, delicious & happy condoms.

CENTER FOR
Sex & Sundhed
www.sexogsundhed.dk

3 exciting, delicious & happy condoms.

CENTER FOR
Sex & Sundhed
www.sexogsundhed.dk

PROJECT
more sex
DESIGNER
mads jakob poulsen
robert daniel nagy
CLIENT
sex and health
denmark

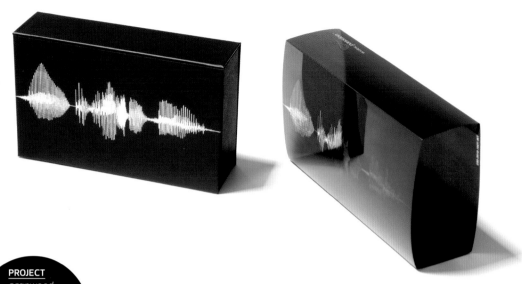

PROJECT
scanwood
DESIGNER
mads jakob poulsen
CLIENT
scanwood

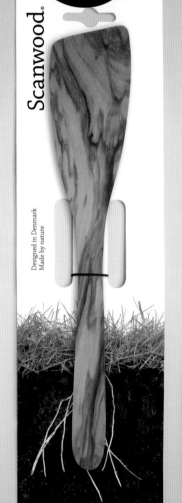

Scanwood.

Designed in Denmark
Made by nature

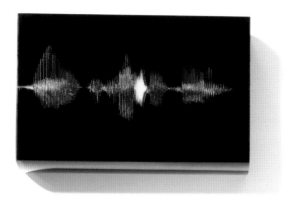

PROJECT
widex
DESIGNER
*mads jakob
poulsen*
CLIENT
*widex hearing
aids*

country
<u>DENMARK</u>

CITY **PROJECT**
egaa *redesigning*
STUDIO *model kits*
kenn munk **DESIGNER**
kenn munk
CLIENT
self initiated

country
DENMARK

CITY **PROJECT**
copenhagen hartmann highlights
STUDIO cd cover / flyer
11design **DESIGNER**
11design
CLIENT
gerl records
büchert
bentzon

FRANCE

46°00` NORTH / 2°00` EAST

FR

country
FRANCE

CITY **PROJECT**
paris *samuel beckett*
STUDIO **DESIGNER**
atelier 25 *capucine*
merkenbrack
chloé tercé
CLIENT
not published
yet

PROJECT
carte de voeux
bazaar d'étoiles
DESIGNER
capucine
merkenbrack
chloé tercé
CLIENT
bazaar d'étoiles

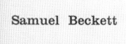

country
FRANCE

CITY
roissy
en brie
STUDIO
samy halim

PROJECT
riz golo
DESIGNER
samy halim
CLIENT
self initiated

PROJECT
diwine
black edition
DESIGNER
samy halim
CLIENT
self initiated

PROJECT
*pantone home
paint*
DESIGNER
samy halim
CLIENT
self initiated

GERMANY

51°00` NORTH / 9°00` EAST

DE

country
GERMANY

CITY **PROJECT**
berlin *borgmann 1772*
STUDIO **DESIGNER**
fons *fons hickmann*
hickmann **CLIENT**
m 23 *borgmann&*
clausen gmbh
borgmann
1772

PROJECT
red dot yearbook
of communication
design 2010 / 11
DESIGNER
fons hickmann
lena gruschka
thomas kronbichler
CLIENT
semperoper dresden

PROJECT
voucher set
semper oper
DESIGNER
fons hickmann
susann stefanizen
CLIENT
semper oper dresden

country
<u>GERMANY</u>

CITY   **PROJECT**
hamburg   food finish
STUDIO   **DESIGNER**
kolle rebbe   kolle rebbe
korefe   korefe
CLIENT
t.d.g.vertriebs
mg&co. kg

FEINER KRAFTSTOFF AUS DER DELI GARAGE: AUSGEZEICHNETER VODKA ABGERUNDET MIT BELEBENDEM ESPRESSO.

THE DELI GARAGE

KRAFTSTOFF
ESPRESSO VODKA

THE DELI GARAGE
FOOD COOPERATIVE

The DeliGarage UG & Co. KG
Alter Wandrahm 10, 20457 Hamburg
WWW.DELI-GARAGE.COM

Inhalte: natürliche Aromen, Alkohol,
Wasser, Zucker.

4 260182 510001   40 % VOL   ⅇ 200 ml

PROJECT
power fuel
DESIGNER
kolle rebbe
korefe
CLIENT
t.d.g.vertriebs
mg&co. kg

THE DELI GARAGE

KRAFTSTOFF
MELONE MINZE VODKA

HOCHWERTIGER KRAFTSTOFF AUS DER DELI GARAGE: PURER VODKA VEREDELT MIT FRUCHTIGER MELONE UND FRISCHER MINZE.

THE DELI GARAGE
FOOD COOPERATIVE

The DeliGarage UG
(haftungsbeschränkt) & Co. KG
Alter Wandrahm 10, 20457 Hamburg

WWW.DELI-GARAGE.COM

Inhalte: natürliche Aromen, Alkohol,
Wasser, Zucker.

4 260182 510001   40 % VOL   ⅇ 200 ml

THE DELI GARAGE

KRAFTSTOFF
INGWER KORIANDER VODKA

EXKLUSIVER KRAFTSTOFF AUS DER DELI GARAGE: FEINSTER VODKA VERFEINERT MIT EINEM HAUCH INGWER UND KORIANDER.

THE DELI GARAGE
FOOD COOPERATIVE

The DeliGarage UG & Co. KG
Alter Wandrahm 10, 20457 Hamburg

WWW.DELI-GARAGE.COM

Inhalte: natürliche Aromen, Alkohol, Wasser, Zucker.

4260182510025

40 % VOL ℮ **200 ml**

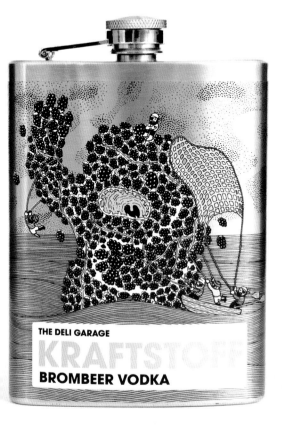

THE DELI GARAGE

KRAFTSTOFF
BROMBEER VODKA

RAFFINIERTER KRAFTSTOFF AUS DER DELI GARAGE: BESTER VODKA MIT FRUCHTIGEN BROMBEEREN.

THE DELI GARAGE
FOOD COOPERATIVE

The DeliGarage UG
(haftungsbeschränkt) & Co. KG
Alter Wandrahm 10, 20457 Hamburg

WWW.DELI-GARAGE.COM

Inhalte: natürliche Aromen, Alkohol, Wasser, Zucker.

4260182510216

40 % VOL ℮ **200 ml**

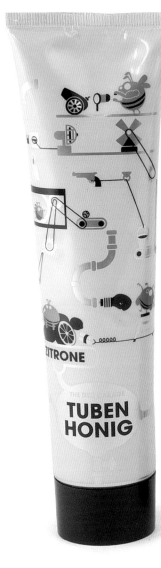

THE DELI GARAGE

TUBENHONIG
SCHOKO · ZITRONE · ZIMT

THE DELI GARAGE
FOOD COOPERATIVE

PROJECT
honey tube
DESIGNER
kolle rebbe
korefe
CLIENT
t.d.g.vertriebs
mg&co. kg

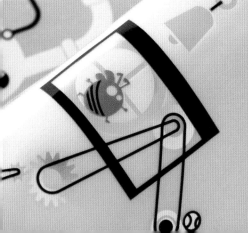

THE DELI GARAGE
ÖLWECHSE
ZITRONE

THE DELI GARAGE

ÖLWECHSEL
PEPERONI · ZITRONE · ROSMARIN

THE DELI GARAGE
FOOD COOPERATIVE

THE DELI GARAGE

ÖLWECHSEL
PEPERONI

THE DELI GARAGE

ÖLWECHSEL
ROSMARIN

PROJECT
oilchange
DESIGNER
kolle rebbe
korefe
CLIENT
t.d.g.vertriebs
mg&co. kg

GARAGE

WEC

ERONI

PROJECT
multi noodles
DESIGNER
kolle rebbe
korefe
CLIENT
t.d.g.vertriebs
mg&co. kg

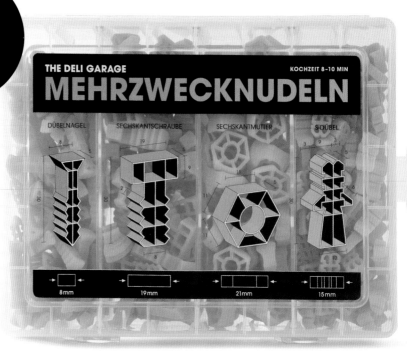

THE DELI GARAGE

SCH
OKO
LEIM

THE DELI GARAGE

SCH
OKO
LEIM

MIT KEKS

PROJECT
chocolate glue
DESIGNER
kolle rebbe
korefe
CLIENT
t.d.g.vertriebs
mg&co. kg

SCH
OKO
LEIM

MIT
KEKS

PROJECT
borkebjs
DESIGNER
kolle rebbe korefe
CLIENT
borkebjs books

Wir leben unter euch versteckt.
Hast du uns schon entdeckt?

ANTHONY'S
GOLDMARIE
ANTHONY'S
MINI GARAGE WINERY
ANTHONY ROBERT HAMMOND

ANTHONY'S
ROT BART
ANTHONY'S
GARAGE WINERY

ANTHONY'S
ROSA MUNDE
ANTHONY'S
GARAGE WINERY
ANTHONY ROBERT HAMMOND

PROJECT
grape battery
DESIGNER
kolle rebbe korefe
CLIENT
t.d.g.vertriebs mg&co. kg

Folge dem letzten Borkebie in das Reich der Fantasie.

country
GERMANY

CITY   **PROJECT**
berlin   *delbo – havarien*
STUDIO   **DESIGNER**
zwölf   *stefan guzy*
         marcus lisse
         björn wiede
         CLIENT
         loob musik

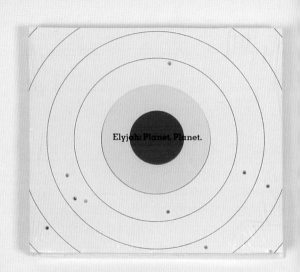

PROJECT
elyjah: planet, planet
DESIGNER
stefan guzy
marcus lisse
björn wiede
CLIENT
klimbim records

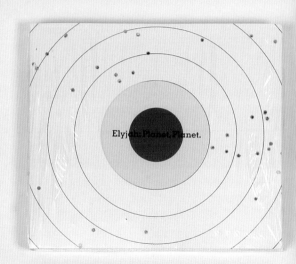

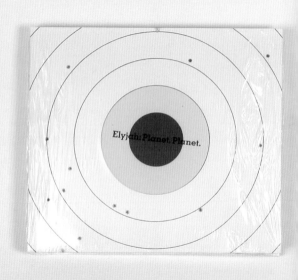

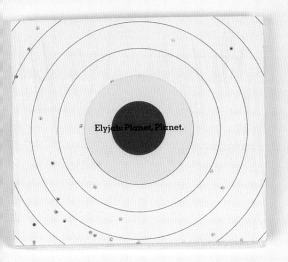

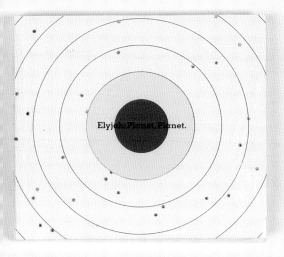

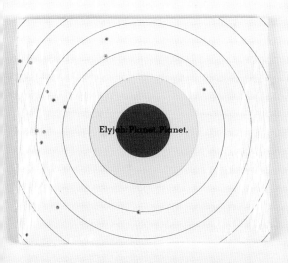

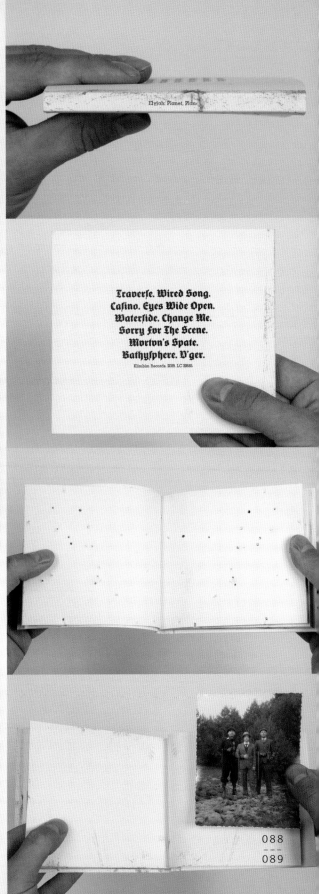

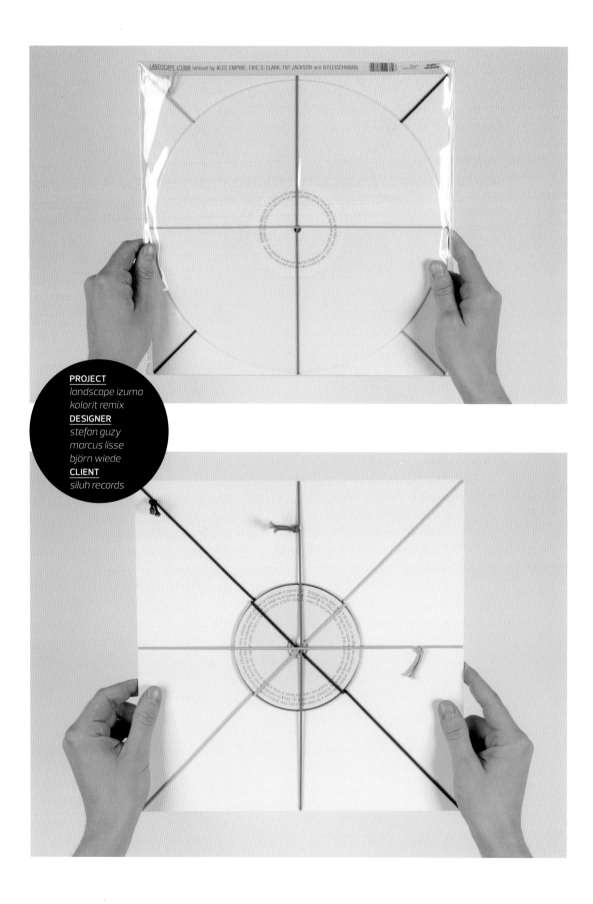

PROJECT
*landscape izuma
kolorit remix*
DESIGNER
*stefan guzy
marcus lisse
björn wiede*
CLIENT
siluh records

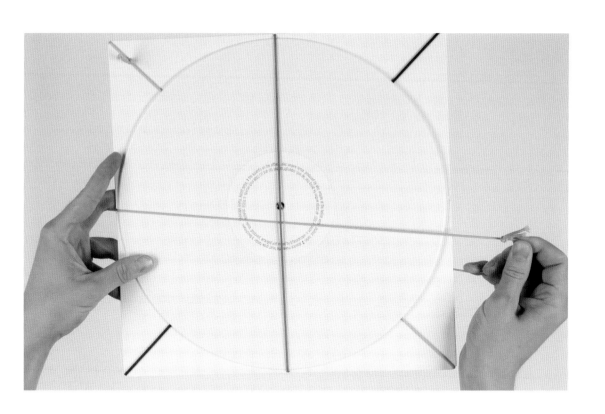

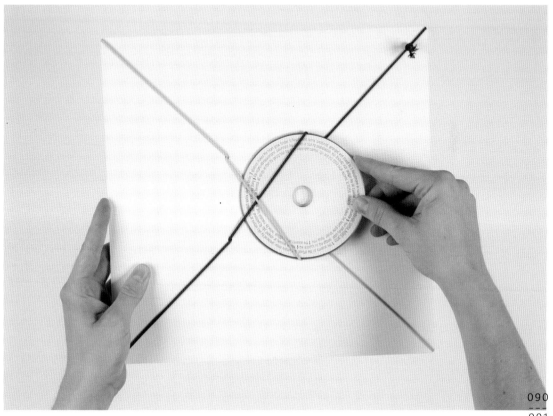

GREECE

31°00'NORTH / 22°00'EAST

GR

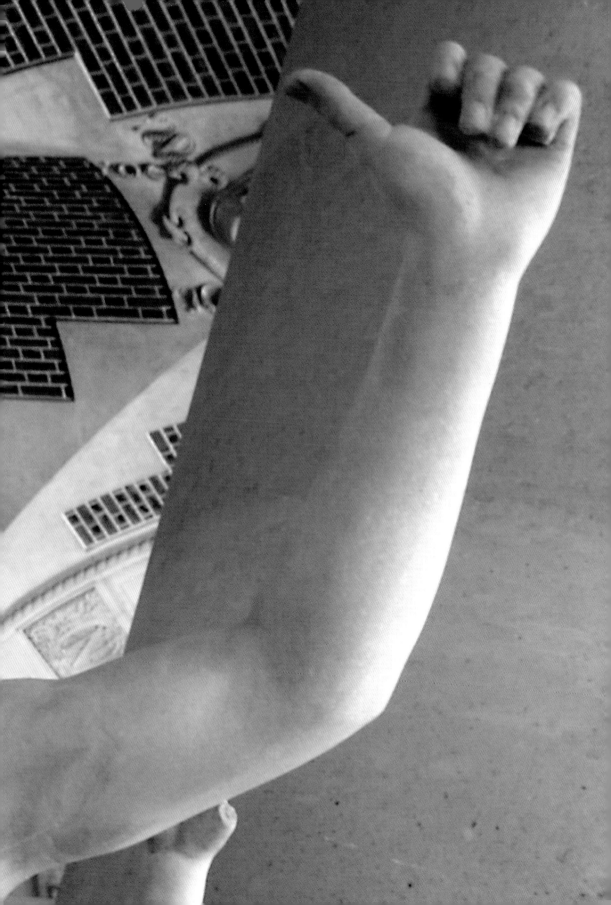

country
GREECE

CITY   **PROJECT**
thessaloniki   *"votrys"*
STUDIO   *wine gift box*
athanasios   **DESIGNER**
babalis   *athanasios babalis*
CLIENT
domaine
gerovasilliov

country
GREECE
CITY **PROJECT**
athens coasters
STUDIO **DESIGNER**
chris trivizas l chris trivizas
design **CLIENT**
paperkingdom

σου
βέρ

coasters

ΧΑΡΤΟΒΑΣΙΛΕΙΟΝ
PAPERKINGDOM
®

PROJECT
shower cap
DESIGNER
chris trivizas
CLIENT
use it

PROJECT
card game
DESIGNER
chris trivizas
CLIENT
perrakis papers

είπε το...ναι;

θα ανοίξει το τενεκεδόκι για να μας

PROJECT
did she say yes?
DESIGNER
chris trivizas
CLIENT
*costas & maria
contou*

country
GREECE

CITY   PROJECT
athens   i cover
STUDIO   DESIGNER
k2 design   anna thanassoula
         CLIENT
         kix solutions

icover® nanotechnology

Inox & Chrome
Προστασία ανοξείδωτων
και επιχρωμιωμένων
επιφανειών. Κάνει το
καθάρισμα παιχνίδι.

Home   250ml

icover® nanotechnology

Inox & Chrome
Προστασία των
ανοξείδωτων επιφανειών
του σκάφους από λεκέδ
δαχτυλιές, άλατα.

Marine   250ml

icover® nanotechnology

Paint Coat B
Σφράγιση και προστασία
στα βημμένα τμήματα το
αυτοκινήτου. Κάνει το
καθάρισμα παιχνίδι.

Car   250ml

icover® nanotechnology

**Protection
Textile Natural**
Προστατεύει τα υφάσμα
και εμποδίζει τη μετάδοσ
της φωτιάς.

Fire   250ml

COSMOS
ΑΚΡΥΛΙΚΟ
ΕΠΑΓΓΕΛΜΑΤΙΚΟ
ACRYLIC PROFESSIONAL

Με ενσωματωμένο σκαφάκι

COSMOS
ACRYL PROFIT

Οικονομικό ακρυλικό χρώμα για επιφάνειες που χρειάζονται συχνή επαναβαφή και φρεσκάρισμα. Δουλεύεται εύκολα, στεγνώνει γρήγορα και έχει μεγάλη καλυπτικότητα και ισχυρή πρόσφυση.

LOW COST ACRYLIC PAINT FOR EXTERIOR USE, SUITABLE FOR SURFACES WHERE FREQUENT PAINTING AND FRESHENING UP IS NEEDED. IT HAS GREAT WORKING PROPERTIES, GREAT HIDING POWER, STRONG ADHESION AND FAST DRYING.

10lt

COVERAGE 8-10m²/lt · WATER DILUTION 5-10% · VOC COMPLIANT

COVERAGE 8-10 m²/lt

COSMOS
ΜΟΝΩΤΙΚΟ ΤΑΡΑΤΣΩΝ
ROOF COATING

Με ενσωματωμένο σκαφάκι

COSMOS
WATERSTOP

Εξαιρετικής ποιότητας ελαστομερές στεγανοποιητικό μονωτικό βασισμένο σε ειδικές ακρυλικές ρητίνες, οι οποίες προσδίδουν μεγάλες αντοχές στην UV ακτινοβολία, στις δύσκολες καιρικές συνθήκες, υψηλή ελαστικότητα ακόμη και σε χαμηλές θερμοκρασίες και εξαιρετική υδροφοβικότητα. Η σύσταση του προϊόντος το καθιστά ιδανικό στις έντονες καιρικές μεταβολές, κυρίως φθάν να στεγανοποιούν αποτελεσματικά τις ρηγματώσεις, για αυτό είναι ιδανικό για μόνωση ταρατσών, βεραντών και τριχοειδών ρωγμών. Έχει άριστη πρόσφυση πάνω σε τσιμέντα, σοβάδες, πλάκες ταρατσών, τούβλα και κάθε οικοδομικό υλικό.

EXCELLENT QUALITY WATERPROOFING AND INSULATING MATERIAL, BASED ON SPECIAL ACRYLIC RESINS, WHICH GIVE STRONG RESISTANCE TO ADVERSE WEATHER CONDITIONS AND UV EXPOSURE. IT HAS HIGH ELASTICITY EVEN IN LOW TEMPERATURES. IT IS SUITABLE FOR WATER SEALING ROOF TERRACES, PATIOS, CAPILLARY CRACKS AND CAN BE APPLIED TO ANY BUILDING MATERIAL.

10lt

COVERAGE 1m²/lt · WATER DILUTION · VOC COMPLIANT

COVERAGE 10-12m²/lt · WATER DILUTION 5-10% · VOC COMPLIANT

PROJECT
cosmos paint
emulsions
DESIGNER
alexis marinis
CLIENT
cosmos lac

COSMOS
ΑΚΡΥΛΙΚΟ/ACRYLIC

Με ενσωματωμένο
σκαφάκι

COSMOS
ACRYL ACRYL

Ακρυλικό με βάση ακρυλικά γαλακτώματα, εξαιρετικό καλυπτικό και ιδιαίτερα λευκά.
Έχει μεγάλη πρόσφυση σε νέες και παλιές επιφάνειες από μπετόν, τούβλα, σοβά,
γυψοσανίδες κ.λ.π. Έχει πολύ καλή αντοχή στις δύσκολες καιρικές συνθήκες
και στην έντονη ηλιακή ακτινοβολία.

SPECIAL FORMULATED ACRYLIC PAINT BASED ON ACRYLIC EMULSIONS. GIVES HIGH COVERAGE
AND EXCEPTIONAL WHITENESS. IT HAS GREAT ADHESION ON NEW AND OLD SURFACES
OF PLASTER, CONCRETE, BRICKS, WOOD, ALONG WITH GREAT RESISTANCE TO ADVERSE WEATHER
CONDITIONS AND UV LIGHT EXPOSURE.

COVERAGE 10-12m²/lt | WATER DILUTION 5-10% | VOC COMPLIANT

10lt

COSMOS
ΑΣΤΙΚΟ ΧΡΩΜΑ
ULSION PAINT

Με ενσωματωμένο
σκαφάκι

COSMOS
PRO

ιτικό ματ πλαστικό χρώμα, καλυπτικό, μεγάλης αντοχής, για εσωτερική χρήση.
λλληλο για επιφάνειες από σοβά, μπετόν, νοβιλάν κ.λ.π.

AL MAT EMULSION PAINT WITH GREAT HIDING POWER FOR INTERIOR USE.
LE FOR PLASTER, CONCRETE, BRICKS, WOOD.

COSMOS
ΠΛΑΣΤΙΚΟ ΧΡΩΜΑ
EMULSION PAINT

Με ενσωματωμένο
σκαφάκι

COSMOS
PLUS PLUS

Εξαιρετικής ποιότητας και καλυπτικότητας χρώμα κατάλληλο για εσωτερική και εξωτερική
χρήση με υψηλές αντοχές στις καιρικές συνθήκες. Η βάση του είναι συμπολυμερές ρητίνες
και υψηλά αρίστης ποιότητας. Συνδυάζει λεία βελούδινη επιφάνεια, με την εξαιρετική λευκότητα.
Απλά στο δούλεμα, έχει μεγάλη καλυπτικότητα και απόδοση ανάλογα με την απορροφητικότητα
της επιφάνειας. Μπορεί να εφαρμοστεί σε μπετόν, σοβά, ξύλα, τούβλα, νοβοσανίδες.

SUPERIOR QUALITY PAINT FOR INTERIOR AND EXTERIOR USE, WITH GREAT HIDING POWER AND OUTSTAND-
ING RESISTANCE IN WEATHER CONDITIONS. BASED ON HIGH QUALITY RAW MATERIALS. RESULTS TO
A SMOOTH AND VELVET SURFACE WITH EXCEPTIONAL WHITENESS. IT HAS GREAT WORKING PROPERTIES,
HIGH COVERAGE AND HIGH SPREADING RATES DEPENDING ON THE SURFACE ABSORPTION CAPACITY.
IT IS SUITABLE FOR PLASTER, CONCRETE, BRICKS, WOOD.

COVERAGE 10-12m²/lt | WATER DILUTION 5-10% | VOC COMPLIANT

10lt

PROJECT
ice creams
DESIGNER
margarita nikitani
yannis kanvandis
CLIENT
kayak

PROJECT
*korres natural
products*
DESIGNER
*chrisafis chrisafis
alexis marinis
dimitra drananti*
CLIENT
*korres natural
products*

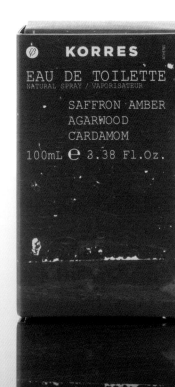

SAFFRON AMBER
AGARWOOD
CARDAMOM

100mL ℮ 3.38 Fl.Oz.
EAU DE TOILETTE

KORRES

EAU DE TOILETTE

ROSE WOOD
BLACKCURRANT
CYCLAMEN

100mL ℮ 3.38 Fl.Oz.

ROSE WOOD
BLACKCURRANT
CYCLAMEN

100mL ℮ 3.38 Fl.Oz.
EAU DE TOILETTE

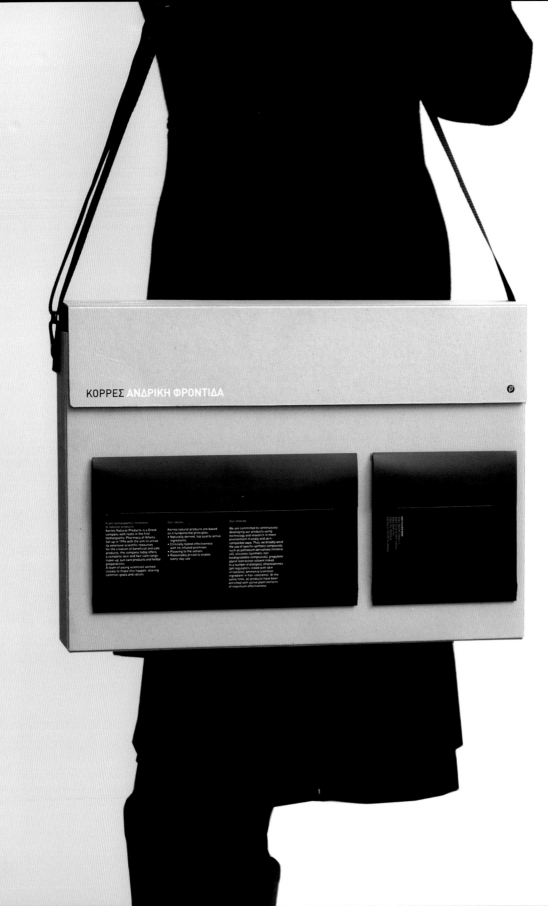

PROJECT
*korres natural
products*
DESIGNER
*chrisafis chrisafis
alexis marinis
dimitra drananti*
CLIENT
*korres natural
products*

PROJECT
korres natural products
DESIGNER
*chrisafis chrisafis
alexis marinis
dimitra drananti*
CLIENT
korres natural products

KORRES

Βανίλια
δαμάσκηνο
αφρόλουτρο
με βιολογικά
εκχυλίσματα
απο αλθαία
και ελίχρυσο

Vanilla
plum
showergel
with organic
extracts
of althea
& helichrysum

90.7% Natural content
NO Parabens_NO Silicones_NO Phthalates

ΒΟΤΑΝΑ/ΣΥΝΕΡΓΑΣΙΕΣ/ΕΚΧΥΛΙΣΕΙΣ/ΕΡΕ

KORRES

Άρκευθος & ρούμι
αφρόλουτρο

Juniper & rum
showergel

Με βιολογικά εκχυλίσματα
από Αλθαία και Ελίχρυσο

HERBS/COOPERATIONS/EXTRACTIONS/RESEARCH

KORRES

Άρκευθος
& ρούμι
αφρόλουτρο
με βιολογικά
εκχυλίσματα
απο αλθαία
και ελίχρυσο

Juniper & rum
showergel
with organic
extracts
of althea
& helichrysum

88% Natural content
NO Parabens_NO Silicones_NO Phthalates

PROJECT
korres natural
products
DESIGNER
chrisafis chrisafis
alexis marinis
dimitra drananti
CLIENT
korres natural
products

"RAKOMELO",
A WARMING
SPIRIT-WITH-
HONEY
CONCOCTION,

KORRESNATURALPRODUCTS

ATHENS
LONDON
NEW YORK
TOKYO
GLASGOW
BARCELONA
MADRID
HELSINKI
PARIS
FRANKFURT
BEIJING
ISTANBUL

From homeopathic remedies to natural products

Korres natural products is a Greek company with roots in the first Homeopathic Pharmacy of Athens. The first Korres product was an aromatic herbal syrup with honey and aniseed, a recipe inspired by "rakomelon", a warming spirit-with-honey concoction, which George Korres' grandfather used to favour in his hometown on the island of Naxos. The company today offers more than 500 skin and hair care products, at leading department stores and 20 stand alone stores, in 28 countries around the world. **Our values** Korres natural products are based on 4 fundamental principles: • Naturally derived, top quality active ingredients. • Clinically tested effectiveness with no inflated promises. • Pleasing to the senses. • Reasonably priced to enable every-day use. **The syntheses** There are four types of active herbal ingredients that we use in our syntheses: • Unique herbs of the Greek flora, known for their traditional use: Olive oil, Thymus Honey, Basil, Camomile, Fennel, Sage, Linden, Rosemary, Mastiha • Medicinal herbs (our pharmacy heritage): Aloe vera, St John's Wort, Evening Primrose, Rosa Moschata, Thyme, Calendula, Echinacea, Gingo biloba, Ginseng, Hamamelis • **New advanced herbal ingredients**, the latest outcome of Science in Cosmetology: Hibiscus, Argan, Andiroba, Wild Mango, Mourera fluviatilis, Imperata cylindrica, Sunflower • Food ingredients, incorporated in their natural form into the formulas in order to maintain their properties: real edible Yoghurt and thyme Honey. At the same time we are committed to continuously developing the base of our products using technology and research in more environment friendly and skin-compatible ways. Thus, we broadly avoid the use of specific synthetic compounds (like petroleum derived mineral oils, silicones, propylene glycol, ethanolamines, ammonia etc), replacing them with naturally derived ingredients, such as vegetable oils and aminoacids, that have nourishing properties and are friendly to the skin. **Our cooperations** In cooperation with the sector of Pharmacognosy (Pharmaceutics department, University of Athens), we participate in industrial research development programmes, with the object of utilising herbs of the Greek flora. At the same time, in cooperation with the Chios Mastiha Growers Association we have developed a special product line, based on Mastiha, the invaluable and unique resin of Chios. Moreover, in cooperation with the Cooperative de Safran, we have undertaken the responsibility to create an extensive range of products with Krokos Kozanis, the highest quality existing Saffron.

country
GREECE

CITY · PROJECT
athens · sugarillos
STUDIO · sugar sticks
mouse · DESIGNER
graphics · gregory tsaknakis
· maria karagianni
· CLIENT
· sugarillos s.a.

ένα
κουταλάκι
ζάχαρη

ένα
κουταλάκι
ζάχαρη

ένα
κουταλάκι
ζάχαρη

ένα
κουταλάκι
ζάχαρη

PROJECT
petrocoll
spatula putty
DESIGNER
gregory tsaknakis
aris pasouris
CLIENT
petrocoll s.a.

ένα
κουταλάκι
ζάχαρη

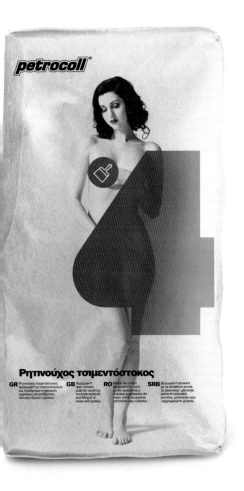

PROJECT
ouzo zarbanis
DESIGNER
gregory tsaknakis
CLIENT
zarbanis s.a.

OU
ZO

100% απόσταγμα ούζου από την οικογένεια
Ζαρμπάνη στη Σάμο. Παραδοσιακή συνταγή
αποτέλεσμα πολύωρης απόσταξης και
μεγάλου χρόνου ωρίμανσης.

ZARBANIS

a greek 100% distilled ouzo from samos
ein Griechische 100% destillierten Ouzo
von Samos.

100%
ΑΠΟΣΤΑΓΜΑ
200ml,42% vol

PROJECT
uncle–statis
frozen herbs
DESIGNER
gregory tsaknakis
aris pasouris
CLIENT
vivartia s.a. frozen
food division

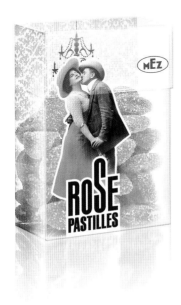

PROJECT
mez/pastilles
DESIGNER
gregory tsaknakis
gina zaafeiraki
CLIENT
lavdas s.a.

ENJOY LIFE
DO NOT
DRINK &
DRIVE

ΚΤΗΜΑ ΣΠΥΡΟΠΟΥΛΟΥ ΓΙΑ ΤΗ ΒΙΟΤΟΣ
CABERNET MERLOT
ΟΙΝΟΣ ΕΡΥΘΡΟΣ 2005
απο σταφύλια βιολογικής γεωργίας

12.5% Vol 750 ml ℮

GREEK
EXTRA
VIRGIN
OLIVE
Oil

EXCLUSIVE SELECTION
ILIADA PDO
KALAMATA
PROTECTED DESIGNATION OF ORIGIN
LIMITED EDITION

country
GREECE

CITY   PROJECT
athens   wine label for
STUDIO   wineyard pyrgou
the design vassilissis
shop   DESIGNER
        dyonisos livanis
        CLIENT
        vineyard pyrgu
        vassilissis

λαγουσιά

Επτάλοφος

Sauvign

νική ποικιλία, άριστα προσαρμοσμένη στις ξηροθερμικ
οποιημένη με τις πιο σύγχρονες οινολογικές τεχνικ
ά και ισορροπημένο οίνο.

λίου. Λευκός Ξηρός, 2007
κά λευκά κρέατα, τυριά και φρούτα.
στους 12-14°C.

Όνομα που δόθηκε από την Βασίλισσα Αμαλία στο πρώτο
περιοχής του ηλίου το 1857. Οι καλλιεργούμενες ποικιλ
Merlot, ύστερα από διωδεκάμηνη παλαίωση σε δρύινα βαρ
παχυρό οίνο με σύνθετα άρωμα και μεστή γεύση.

Επιτραπέζιος Οίνος Ιλίου. Ερυθρός Ξηρός, 2006
Συνοδεύει άριστα κόκκινα κρέατα, κυνήγι και ώριμα τυρ
ιδανικές συνθήκες για αρκετά χρόνια. Πίνεται σε θερμ

PROJECT
*georges. extra
virgin olive oil*
DESIGNER
dionysis livanis
CLIENT
*greek olives &
olive oil
company*

georges
SINCE 1691

EXTRA VIRGIN
OLIVE OIL

THE GEORGES FAMILY HAS
BEEN CULTIVATING OLIVE
TREES AT ITS ARFARA FARM
NEAR KALAMATA FOR MORE
THAN 300 YEARS. THIS PURE,
SINGLE VARIETAL KORONEIKI
EXTRA VIRGIN OLIVE OIL
IS THE NATURAL RESULT OF
THESE YEARS OF DEDICATION
AND EXPERIENCE. COMBINING
TRADITIONAL CULTIVATION
METHODS WITH STATE OF THE
ART PRODUCTION TECHNOLOGY,
GEORGES OIL BRINGS TOGETHER
THE ANCIENT AND THE
MODERN TO BRING YOU THE
FINEST SUPERIOR QUALITY
OLIVE OIL. APPRECIATED BY
CONNOISSEURS FOR ITS RICH
COLOUR, FINE AROMA AND
FULL-BODIED TASTE.

georges
SINCE 1691

EXTRA VIRGIN
OLIVE OIL

TRADITIONALLY PRODUCED
AT THE ARFARA FARM
IN KALAMATA, GREECE.

www.georgesolives.com

0.3% MAX ACIDITY

3 L ℮

PROJECT
waks nature
DESIGNER
dionysis livanis
maria kefala
CLIENT
hellenic candle
company

<u>ICELAND</u>

<u>65°00` NORTH / 18°00` WEST</u>

<u>IS</u>

country
ICELAND

CITY
reykjavik

STUDIO
sruli recht

PROJECT
rᶨng sr118

DESIGNER
sruli recht

CLIENT
in-house release

PROJECT
carbon dater sr119
DESIGNER
sruli recht
CLIENT
in-house release

IRELAND

53°00' NORTH / 7°00' EAST

IE

country
IRELAND

CITY PROJECT
dublin new breed
STUDIO DESIGNER
detail detail design studio
design CLIENT
studio emi music ireland

DOUBLE CD FEATURING:
...DES, CATHY DAVEY,
...LORENTOS, MESSIAH J AND
...E EXPERT, MICK FLANNERY
...WO DOOR CINEMA CLUB...

THE
NEW BREED
THE BEST OF NEW IRISH CONTEMPORARY MUSIC

THE NEW BREED

DISC 1

EMI Music Ireland

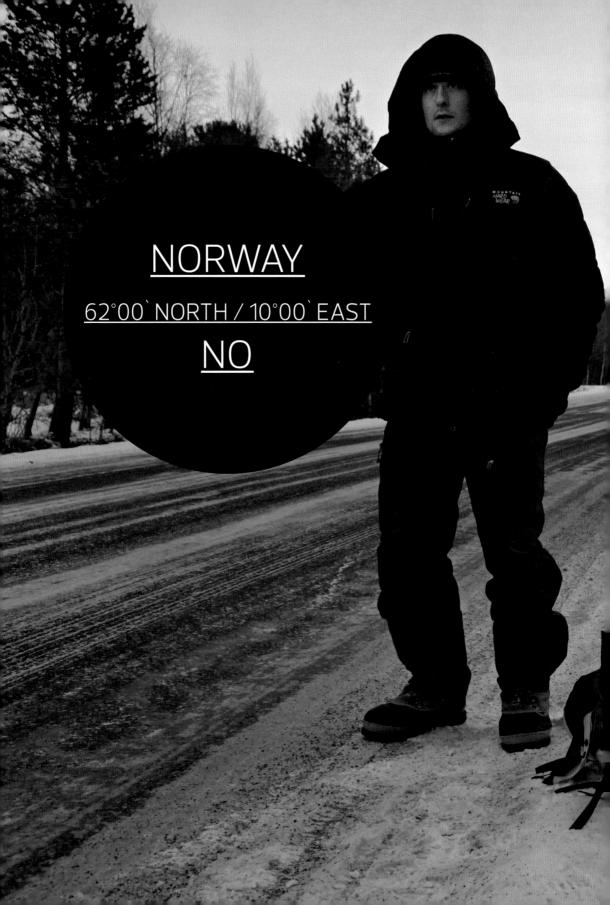

NORWAY

62°00` NORTH / 10°00` EAST

NO

country
NORWAY

CITY **PROJECT**
oslo *wishbox packaging*
STUDIO **DESIGNER**
bleed *astrid feldner*
CLIENT
wishbox
florent asté
wish as

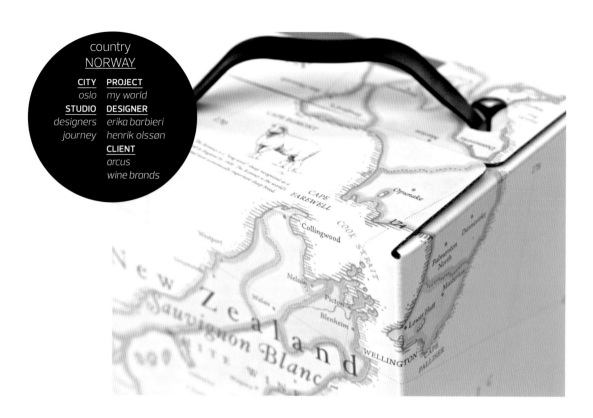

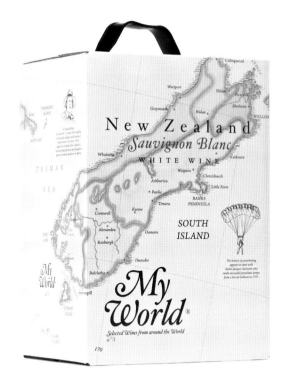

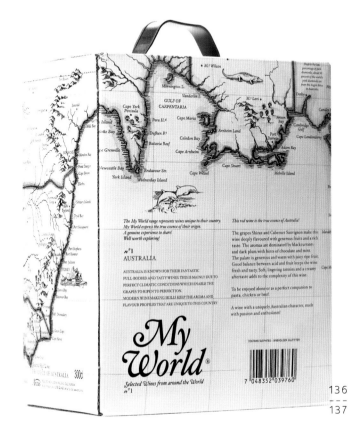

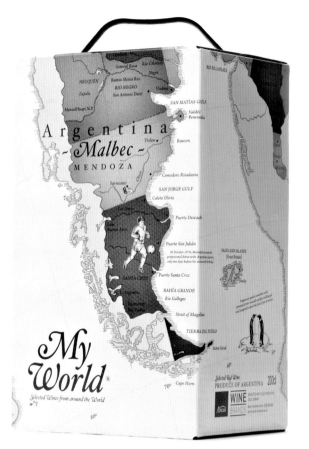

Argentina
~ Malbec ~
MENDOZA

My World®
Selected Wines from around the World
nº2

Selected Red Wine
PRODUCE OF ARGENTINA   200cl

WINE
BRANDS

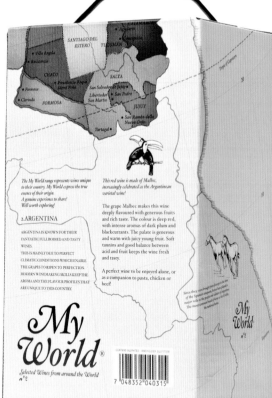

The My World range represents wines unique
to their country. My World express the true
essence of their origin.
A genuine experience to share!
Well worth exploring!

2.ARGENTINA

ARGENTINA IS KNOWN FOR THEIR
FANTASTIC FULL BODIED AND TASTY
WINES.
THIS IS MAINLY DUE TO PERFECT
CLIMATIC CONDITIONS WHICH ENABLE
THE GRAPES TO RIPEN TO PERFECTION.
MODERN WINEMAKING SKILLS KEEP THE
AROMA AND THE FLAVOUR PROFILES THAT
ARE UNIQUE TO THIS COUNTRY.

This red wine is made of Malbec,
increasingly celebrated as the Argentinean
varietal wine!

The grape Malbec makes this wine
deeply flavoured with generous fruits
and rich taste. The colour is deep red,
with intense aromas of dark plum and
blackcurrants. The palate is generous
and warm with juicy young fruit. Soft
tannins and good balance between
acid and fruit keeps the wine fresh
and tasty.

A perfect wine to be enjoyed alone, or
as a companion to pasta, chicken or
beef!

My World®
Selected Wines from around the World
nº2

CONTAINS SULPHITES · INNEHOLDER SULFITTER

7 048352 040315

PROJECT
santé
DESIGNER
erika barbieri
henrik olssøn
CLIENT
arcus wine
brands

Santé
Vin de Pays d'Oc
grape
Cabernet Sauvignon   vintage 10/06

This wine has a deep red colour, a rich fruitcharacter on the nose, with lots of blackcurrants, typical for the grape Cabernet Sauvignon. The taste is medium-bodied, with an integrated tanninstructure and velvety texture. The aftertaste is wellbalanced and lingering. A delightful wine that can hold its own — paired with a meal or enjoyed solo.

SANTÉ IS A MODERN RED WINE FROM THE FRENCH REGION LANGUEDOC-ROUSSILLON. THE WINE IS MADE OF 100% CABERNET SAUVIGNON GRAPES AND IS NATURALLY RICH IN ANTIOXIDANTS. THE ANTIOXIDANTS FOUND IN RED WINE BELONG TO THE POLYPHENOLS, FOUND IN THE SKIN, STEM AND SEEDS OF THE GRAPE.

Total Antioxidant level > 3 mmol/100g   *Produce of France*

T. 5. N°34   *Vitis Vinifera · Wine Grape*

Total Antioxidant level > 3 mmol/100g

Santé
Vin de Pays d'Oc
grape
Cabernet Sauvignon

Selected and filled by Arcus AS, Oslo, Norway.
For more information about antioxidants go to
www.arcus.no

75cl   12,5%vol.
PRODUCE OF FRANCE
contient des sulfites · contains sulphites

olssøn&barb

FINEST
TIMELESS
ACCESSORIES

This bag was assembled by hand in 20.09

PROJECT
olssøn&barbieri
DESIGNER
designers journey
CLIENT
own project

PROJECT
moms
DESIGNER
designers journey
CLIENT
undisclosed

PROJECT
claremont shiraz
DESIGNER
designers journey
CLIENT
arcus wine brands

CLAREMONTSHIRAZ
WESTERN AUSTRALIA [2005]

The koala only eat Eucalyptus leaves and can sleep up to
twenty hours every day. The first hand-colored sketches of
the koala was provided by the explorer *Matthew Flinder*
(1774–1814) during his expedition from 1801–1805 when
[made the Koala famous
in the 18th Century]
he set out to officially map the Australian Coastline.

Produce of Australia
[Red Wine of Australia]

Claremont Shiraz has a plesantly soft and fruity style, with
complexity of pepper and liquorice, plum and blueberry.
[delicious with
An excellent Shiraz from Western Australia.
beef, lamb and pasta dishes]

Claremont Shiraz har en tiltalende blot og fruktdrevet stil,
med aromaer av pepper og lakris, plommer og blåbær.
[En strålende
ideell til biff, lam og pastaretter,
Shiraz fra western Australia.]

75cl.   [Contains sulphites]
                        13,5%vol.

Selected and
bottled by
Arcus AS, Oslo,
Norway
www.arcus.no   7 048352 025206

CLAREMONT
TRAMINER/RIESLING
SOUTH EASTERN AUSTRALIA

The Kangaroo love to relax in the shadows of the trees
during daytime. Captain James Cook (1728–1779)
[made the Kangaroo famous
discovered the Kangaroo and introduced it to the English
in the 18th Century]
long ago during his first voyage to Australia from 1768-1771.

Produce of Australia
[White Wine of Australia]

Claremont Traminer/Riesling is a pleasant, aromatic white
wine with aromas of apricot, peach and tropical fruits.
[perfect with salads
A fresh semi-dry white wine, from South Eastern Australia,
or simply on its own.]

Claremont Traminer/Riesling er en utpreget aromatisk og
behagelig hvitvin med dominans av aprikos, fersken og
tropisk frukt. Vinen har et delikat innslag av sødme,
kombinert med en tydelig friskhet. Vinen passer perfekt til
lettere friske salater eller kun som forfriskning.

[Contains sulphites]
75cl.   12%vol.

Selected and
bottled by
Arcus AS, Oslo,
Norway
www.arcus.no   7 048351 005711

PROJECT
*claremont traminer
riesling*
DESIGNER
designers journey
CLIENT
arcus wine brands

RABBIT "*Le Lapin*"
the silent member of the...

BARREL "*Le Tonneau*"
If it could talk it would have been the wisest of us.

CHAIR "*La Chaise*"
a refreshing rest in the...

SUNFLOWER "*Le Tournesol*"
they stear at the sun their all life, from morning to night.

À LA
Unforgettable with food
PETITE FERME®
Appellation Madiran Contrôlée
VIN ROUGE
Product de France

CHEESE "*Le Fromage*"
the Tannat wine charm goes with strong, well matured and blue cheeses, like hard Parmesan and Blooming Rind cheese

SEBASTIEN "*Le Chien*"
has the habit of collecting the grapes that miss the pickers baskets.

VEAL "*Le Veau*"
as a general tasting note, Tannat red wine is best paired with strongly flavoured dishes

CHESS "*Les Échecs*"
when your legs are tired, it's time to let your mind go to work.

PROJECT
as it should be
DESIGNER
designers journey
CLIENT
arcus wine brands

PROJECT
siglo de oro
DESIGNER
designers journey
CLIENT
arcus wine brands

PROJECT
herregårds gløgg
DESIGNER
designers journey
CLIENT
arcus wine brands

PROJECT
moel
DESIGNER
designers journey
CLIENT
arcus wine brands

PROJECT
atlungstad aquavit
DESIGNER
designers journey
CLIENT
arcus as

PROJECT
lysholm sydd aquavit
DESIGNER
designers journey
CLIENT
arcus as

PROJECT
milestone
DESIGNER
designers journey
CLIENT
arcus wine brands

2006
DRY WHITE WINE

MILESTONE
Oaked Chardonnay

South Eastern Australia

...estone Oaked Chardonnay
...rvested from the coolest
...neards of South Eastern Australia.
... naturally rich and elegant
...l gives this wine excellent

aromatic expression and ha...
concentration. With a perfect crisp...
freshness and a well integrated oa...
character, this wine is eas...
enjoyed. Milestone - sheer pleasur...

PRODUCT OF AUSTRALIA   13,5%vol.

2007

MILESTONE
Semillon · Sauvignon Blanc

South Africa

...estone is made from the grapes
...illon and Sauvignon Blanc that
... harvested in vineyards of the
...h Eastern Cape.
...rvested gives a fresh, fruity taste

to this wine together with a...
excellent harmonious taste o...
aromatic fruit. This wine has a ...
balanced mixture of fruits and can...
easily be enjoyed.

PRODUCT OF SOUTH AFRICA   12,5%vol.

country
NORWAY

CITY   **PROJECT**
oslo   zubrówka vodka
STUDIO   design suggestion
limi   **DESIGNER**
design   elisabeth limi
CLIENT
rmit university,
melbourne
australia

žubrówka

POLMOS BIALYSTOK GORZELNIE

PREMII POLSKIE WÓDKI

60%

INFUSED WITH HIEROCHLOE ODORATA   60% vol. ℮650mL

DRINK RESPONSIBLY
Product of Poland.
Imported by ASM Liquor
www.asmaliquor.com

STANDARD
DRINKS
20

9 300663 271665

country
NORWAY

CITY **PROJECT**
oslo arctic candy
STUDIO **DESIGNER**
neue lars havard
design dahlstrom
studio jostein sanderson
CLIENT
arctic candy

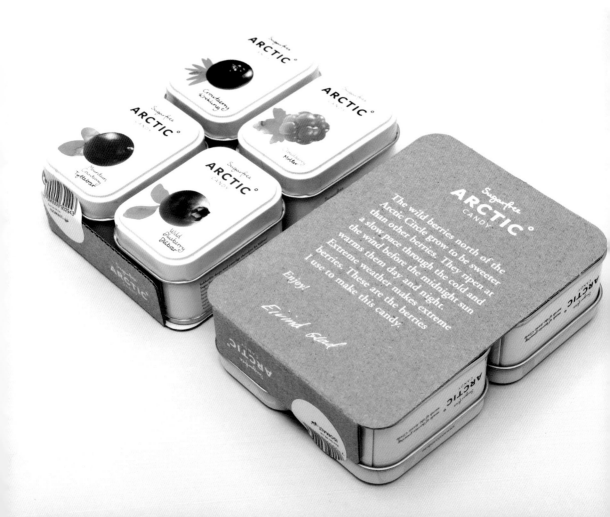

PROJECT
pure identity redesign
DESIGNER
lars havard dahlstrom
benjamin stenmarck
oystein haugseth
CLIENT
the pure water co

PORTUGAL

39°30` NORTH / 8°00` WEST

PT

country
PORTUGAL

CITY **PROJECT**
lisbon *cem amigos*
STUDIO *hundred friends*
musa **DESIGNER**
work lab *musa work lab*
CLIENT
logo wines

VINHO REGIONAL
ALENTEJANO
PORTUGAL

CEM AMIGOS
2007

VINHO REGIONAL
ALENTEJANO
PORTUGAL

CEM AMIGOS
Reserva 2007

PROJECT
blossom
soap box and cd case
DESIGNER
musa work lab
CLIENT
fashion clinic

PROJECT
hg oil
DESIGNER
musa work lab
CLIENT
herdade grande

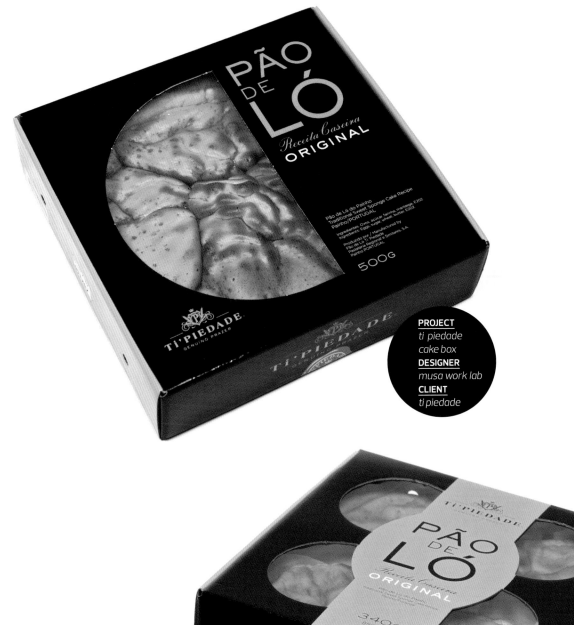

PROJECT
ti piedade
cake box
DESIGNER
musa work lab
CLIENT
ti piedade

PROJECT
the pack 01
DESIGNER
musa work lab
CLIENT
musa collective

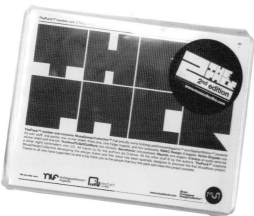

PROJECT
*grey goose vodka
press kit*
DESIGNER
musa work lab
CLIENT
*bacardi–martini
portugal*

GREY GOOSE
World's Best Tasting Vodka

SABE GUARDAR UM SEGREDO?

Sempre que descubro algo que deixa os meus sentidos em êxtase,
juro a mim próprio guardar segredo. Afinal, uma das regras de ouro
dos apreciadores das coisas boas da vida é não partilharem o segredo
de uma nova descoberta com mais ninguém.

Mas se precisasse de uma boa desculpa para quebrar os meus
princípios, ela não podia ser melhor. Descobri a melhor vodka do
mundo - Grey Goose Vodka - e não resisto a revelá-la ao mundo,
mundo este que suspeito não me perdoaria quando descobrisse o
que eu lhe estava a esconder.

Descubra-o aqui.

Seja responsável. Beba com moderação.

PROJECT
imagina (imagine)
packagings
DESIGNER
musa work lab
CLIENT
cnoti portugal

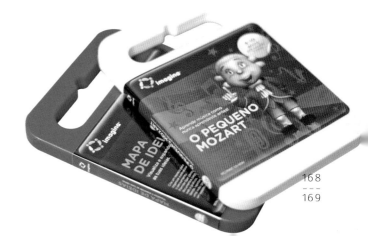

PROJECT
*william lawson's
christmas packaging*
DESIGNER
musa work lab
CLIENT
*bacardi–martini
portugal*

FINEST BLENDED

ESTᴰ 1849

WILLIAM
LAWSON'S®

SCOTLAND

SCOTCH WHISKY

DISTILLED AND BOTTLED BY

WILLIAM LAWSON
DISTILLERS LTD.

40%vol   *Coatbridge & Macduff*   70cl

BOTTLED IN SCOTLAND

DISTILLED, MATURED AND BOTTLED IN SCOTLAND

WILLIAM LAWSON

WILLIAM
LAWSON'S®

SCOTCH WHISKY

DISTILLED AND BOTTLED BY

WILLIAM LAWSON
DISTILLERS LTD.

Coatbridge & Macduff

W. Lawson's
WILLIAM LAWSON'S
SCOTCH WHISKY

GINJA D'ÓBIDOS

PREMIUM
CHERRY LIQUEUR

19% vol.   500ml

Feito com os melhores frutos,
especialmente escolhidos de forma
a obter um licor puro e aromático
Uma mista de sabores aveludados e
encorpados

Exclusively made with the finest fruit,
specially chosen
to obtain a pure and aromatic liqueur

country
PORTUGAL

CITY   PROJECT
lisbon   ginja d'óbidos
STUDIO   DESIGNER
ntgj   guilherme jardim
packaging&   CLIENT
brand design ginja d'óbidos

PROJECT
balblair scotch whiskey
DESIGNER
guilherme jardim
CLIENT
balblair

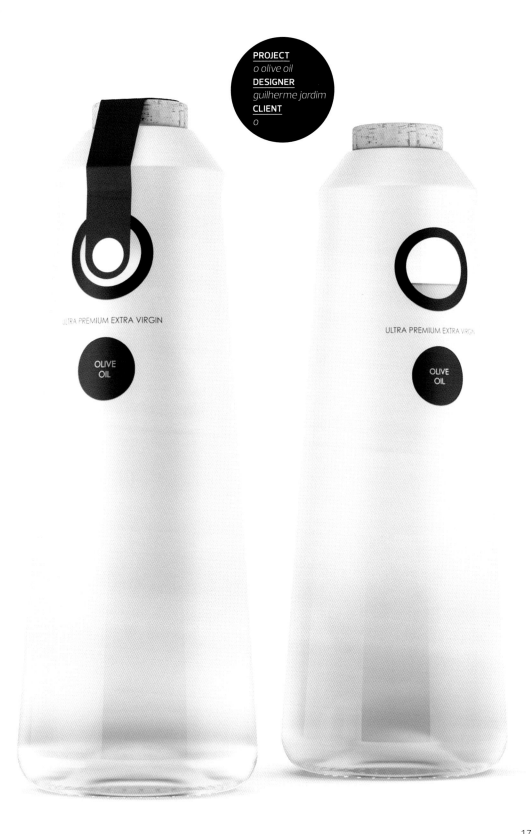

PROJECT
o olive oil
DESIGNER
guilherme jardim
CLIENT
o

ULTRA PREMIUM EXTRA VIRGIN

OLIVE
OIL

ULTRA PREMIUM EXTRA VIRGIN

OLIVE
OIL

PROJECT
karhu beer
DESIGNER
guilherme jardim
CLIENT
*re design of
beer label*

ALC. 5.0% VOL.
330 ML

KARHU
III
ALE

LICOR BEIRÃO

—— PREMIUM ——

LIMITED EDITION
0202/1000

PROJECT
licor beirao
DESIGNER
guilherme jardim
CLIENT
licor beirao

PROJECT
primvs
DESIGNER
guilherme jardim
CLIENT
primvs

P·R·I·M·V·S

STILL
MINERAL WATER
ULTRA LOW SODIUM

P·R·I·M·V·S

STILL
MINERAL WATER
ULTRA LOW SODIUM

P·R·I·M·V·S

SPARKLING
MINERAL WATER
ULTRA LOW SODIUM

P·R·I·M·V·S

SPARKLING
MINERAL WATER
ULTRA LOW SODIUM

P·R·I·M·V·S

OLIO EXTRA VERGINE DI OLIVA
DOP

P·R·I·M·V·S

OLIO EXTRA VERGINE DI OLIVA
DOP

SPAIN

40°00` NORTH / 4°00` WEST

ES

country
SPAIN

CITY   PROJECT
barcelona   2010
STUDIO   DESIGNER
bendita   alba rosell
gloria   santi fuster
CLIENT
casa mariol

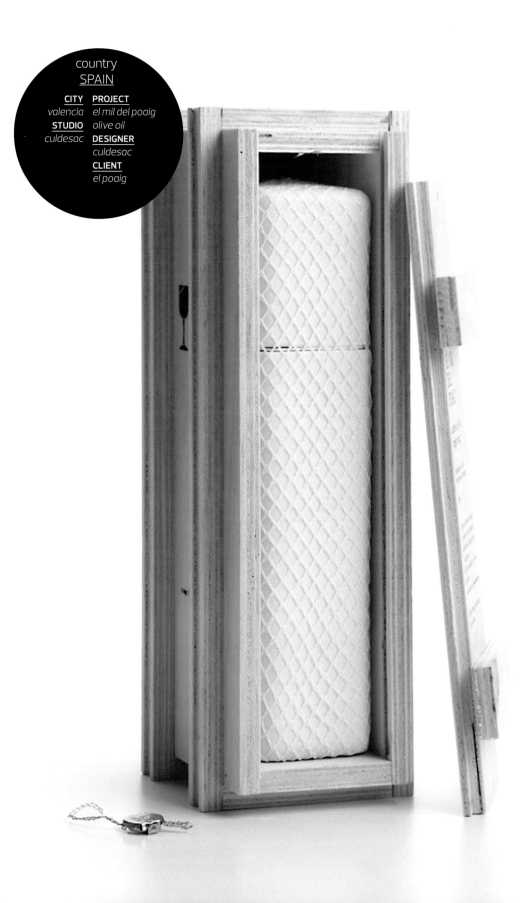

country
SPAIN

CITY **PROJECT**
valencia el mil del poaig
STUDIO olive oil
culdesac **DESIGNER**
culdesac
CLIENT
el poaig

PROJECT
el verd del poaig
DESIGNER
culdesac
CLIENT
el poaig

country
SPAIN

CITY **PROJECT**
barcelona mas romaní
STUDIO **DESIGNER**
gabriel morales gabriel
graphic design morales
and commu- **CLIENT**
nication mas romaní

country
SPAIN

CITY   **PROJECT**
barcelona   womo
STUDIO   **DESIGNER**
ruiz and   david ruiz
company   mercedes cuetos
CLIENT
bread & power

1/2 kg

black and white, tea butter biscuits, capuccino chocolate almond biscuits, lemon biscuits, striped cocoa almond squares, ginger corners, butter hazelnut, fruit tea biscuits, café au lait green tea biscuits

womo

biscuits

cappuccino
chocolate

galletas de mantequilla con café, chocolate y almendras

300 g

sorry

Esto no es una lata de bolitas de chocolate, es una forma de pedirte disculpas, cuatrocientos gramos de disculpas que espero aceptes y disfrutes, una por una.

choco beat

frambuesa, limoncello, almendra red, avellana

400g

womo

bubble
gum

arándano

130g

womo

hanks

cómo darte las gracias. Pero te doy este
leno de bolitas de chocolate, que mereces
o más que cualquier relamido discurso de
ecimiento.

co beat

esa, limoncello,
ra red, avellana

womo

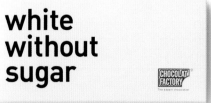
white
without
sugar

black
without
sugar

PROJECT
bars
DESIGNER
david ruiz
CLIENT
*chocolat
factory*

white

80%

milk
without
sugar

70%

grenade

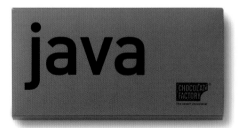
with
caramel

java

with
moka

sao
thome

with
milk

From Madrid
with chocolate

From Barcelona
with chocolate

From Baleares
with chocolate

From Tenerife
with chocolate

PROJECT
the souvenirs
DESIGNER
jorge novedra
vicente ruiz
ainhoa nagore
CLIENT
chocolat factory

THE SOUVENIR FROM MADRID
CHOCOLAT FACTORY

PROJECT
smoothies swell
DESIGNER
ainboa nagore
CLIENT
envasados eva

Swell
SMOOTHIE

the
bottle
of
fruit:

&

THE MOST
HONEST
CHOCOLATE
TABLET

34 Kcal   68 Kcal   102 Kcal   136 Kcal   170 Kcal

PROJECT
the most honest
DESIGNER
vicente ruiz
CLIENT
chocolat factory

PROJECT
lo mon
DESIGNER
ainboa nagore
CLIENT
trossos del priorat

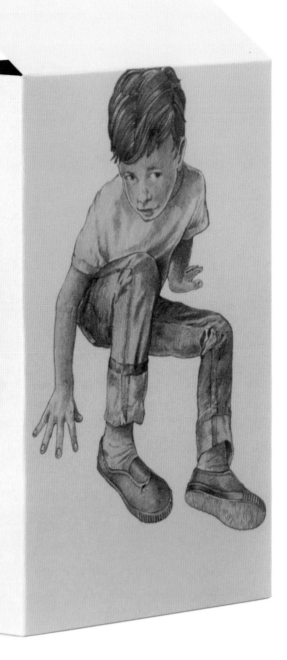

PROJECT
snook pack
DESIGNER
david ruiz
alicic armet
CLIENT
cock a snook

snook®

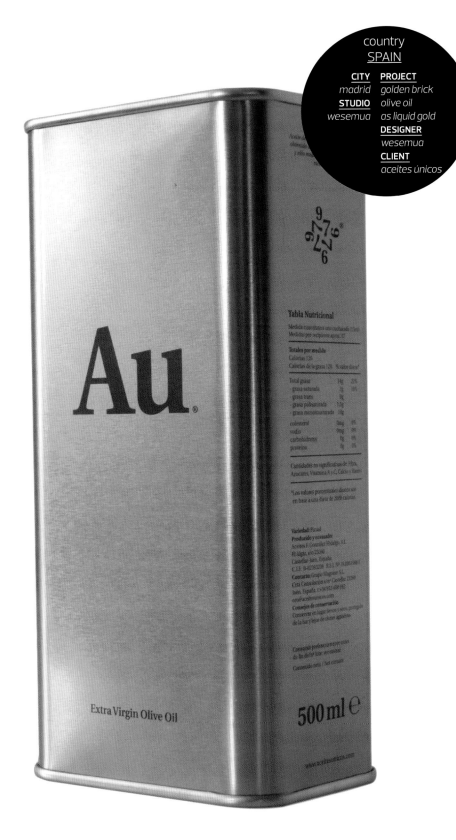

DOUBLE
WORK
DOUBLE
LOVE

TWIN CLOTHING
ropa para gemelos

TOT-a-LOT

JUAN

CRISTINA

TOT-a-LOT

TWICE IN MY LIFE

TWIN CLOTHING
ropa para gemelos

TOT-a-

TERESA

TOT-a-LOT

LUCÍA

DOUBLE
WORK
DOUBLE
LOVE

TWIN CLOTHING
ropa para gemelos

TWICE IN MY LIFE

TWIN CLOTHING
ropa para gemelos

TWICE
UPON
A TIME

PROJECT
use me as drawers
twin clothes
DESIGNER
wesemua
CLIENT
tot–a–lot

SWEDEN

62°00`NORTH / 15°00`EAST

SE

country
SWEDEN

CITY   PROJECT
stockholm   crisp bread
STUDIO   DESIGNER
a–b–d   mikael abbhagen
frederik bengtsson
CLIENT
delights of
sweden

country
SWEDEN

CITY **PROJECT**
stockholm blossa lingo n berry
STUDIO blossa orange light
bvd mulled wine
DESIGNER
bvd
CLIENT
pernod ricard
v&s group

PROJECT
blossa 03–09
DESIGNER
bvd
CLIENT
*pernod ricard
v&s group*

Ultrasilencer
Special Edition
Pia Wallén

PROJECT
*electroloux
ultrasilencer
special edition
pia wallén*
DESIGNER
bvd
CLIENT
electrolux

Thinking of you
Electrolux

Ultrasilencer
Special Edition
Pia Wallén

Thinking of you
Electrolux

PROJECT
absolut ruby red
DESIGNER
bvd
CLIENT
pernod ricard
v&s group

ABSOLUT®
Country of Sweden
RUBY RED

*Immerse yourself in the refreshing
taste of zesty grapefruit, blended with
vodka distilled from grain grown
in the rich fields of southern Sweden.
The distilling and flavoring of vodka
is an age-old Swedish tradition
dating back more than 400 years.
Vodka has been sold under the name
Absolut since 1879.*

40% ALC./VOL. (80 PROOF)   1 LITER
IMPORTED
GRAPEFRUIT FLAVORED VODKA
PRODUCED AND BOTTLED IN ÅHUS, SWEDEN
V&S VIN&SPRIT AB (PUBL)

ABSOLUT®
Country of Sweden
PEARS

*Experience the fruity and
delicate flavor blended with vodka
distilled from grain grown
in the rich fields of southern Sweden.
The distilling and flavoring of vodka
is an age-old Swedish tradition
dating back more than 400 years.
Vodka has been sold under the name
Absolut since 1879.*

40% ALC./VOL. (80 PROOF)   1 LITER
IMPORTED
PEAR FLAVORED VO...
PRODUCED AND BOTTLED IN...
V&S VIN&SPRIT A...

PROJECT
absolut pear
DESIGNER
bvd
CLIENT
pernod ricard
v&s group

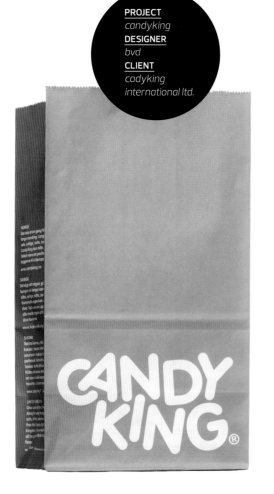

PROJECT
candyking
DESIGNER
bvd
CLIENT
cadyking
international ltd.

PROJECT
lemonaid
DESIGNER
bvd
CLIENT
lemonaid gmbh

ChariTea® black

Schwarzer Tee mit Zitrone, biologisch angebaut und frisch aufgebrüht

country
<u>SWEDEN</u>

CITY **PROJECT**
stockholm *condamine*
STUDIO **DESIGNER**
hanna *hanna*
backman *backman*
CLIENT
condamine

I DET OFÖRSTÖRDA och natur-
sköna Fitou i södra Frankrike
växer druvorna till detta vin
av de, för Fitou, traditionella
druvsorterna *Carignan*, *Grenache*
och *Syrah*. Druvorna växer på
vinstockar och plockas helt och
hållet för hand.
    För att ge vinet en extra dim-
ention lagras en del av vinet i
franska ekfat. Vinet är fylligt,
elegant och välbalanserat och
utmärkt till olika typer av
grytor, gris, vilt samt till ost.

PRODUCT OF FRANCE
750 ML
13,5% VOL.

ISBN 91-89204-38-7

9 789189 204386

country
SWEDEN

CITY · PROJECT
malmö · brie bistro
STUDIO · DESIGNER
id · emma ringsberg
communication · per hallin, golvet
· CLIENT
· skånemejerier

country
SWEDEN

CITY　**PROJECT**
stockholm　*white label*
STUDIO　*series*
liedgren　**DESIGNER**
design　*liedgren design*
　CLIENT
　åkesson vin
　sweden

ÅKESSON

OZ ROZZ

FRISKT ROSÉVIN
AUSTRALIEN
12,5% vol. 1 LITER

ÅKESSON

OZ ROZZ

FRISKT ROSÉVIN
AUSTRALIEN
12,5% vol. 250 ml

country
SWEDEN

CITY   **PROJECT**
stockholm   *tunga varumärken*
STUDIO   **DESIGNER**
pangea   *frederik andersson*
design ab   *örjan nordling*
CLIENT
peter pluntky

country
SWEDEN

CITY **PROJECT**
stockholm kronvodka
STUDIO **DESIGNER**
neumeister peter neumeister
strategic mattias lindstedt
design ab tobias andersson
CLIENT
kronvodka

V
KRONVODKA
För kronobrännerierna var bara det
bästa gott nog. Kronvodka görs på finaste
höstvete och fatlagrad kornsprit. Det ger en
ren, rund och mjuk smak. Med sin tydliga
karaktär är den perfekt för en vodka
martini. Eller drick den som den är.
Med en isbit eller två.

40% vol   350 ml

17
76
KRONVODKA
Endast synnerligen utsökt
kvalitet kunde vinna svensk-
arnas uppskattning. Det insåg
GUSTAV III när den första
buteljen lämnade kronobrän-
neriet 1776. En kvalitet som
har förfinats genom seklerna.

40% vol
350 ml

V&S   VSGROUP.COM
V&S VIN & SPRIT AB (PUBL), SE-117 97 STOCKHOLM

Grouse

Hunting

Superior Performance Cartridge

Pcs **25** / Cal **12** / mm **70** / g 3
Plastic Case / Smokeless Powde
Plastic Low Friction Wad / High C

Pheasant

Hunting

Superior Performance Cartridges

Pcs **25** / Cal **12** / mm **65** / g **30** / US €
Paper Case / Smokeless Powder / Star Cr
odegradeable Fibre Wad / Diamond Lea

GYTTORP
Precision by Tradition

p
Shot

GYTTORP
Precision by Tradition

GYTTORP
Precision by Tradition

Special
Hunting

Superior Performance Cartridges

Pcs **10** / Cal **12** / mm **70** / g **36** / US **1**
Plastic Case / Smokeless Powder / Star Crimp
Plastic Low Friction Wad / High Grade Lead Shot

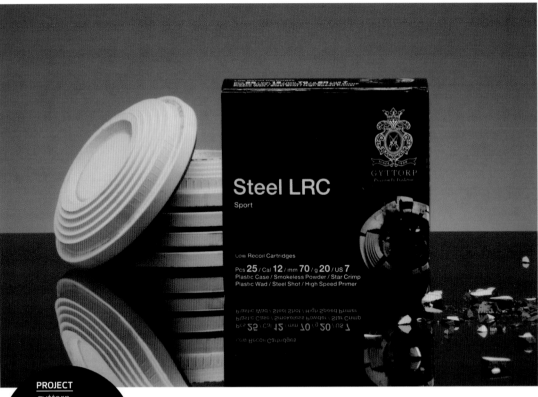

PROJECT
gyttorp
DESIGNER
peter neumeister
mattias lindstedt
tobias andersson
CLIENT
gyttorp

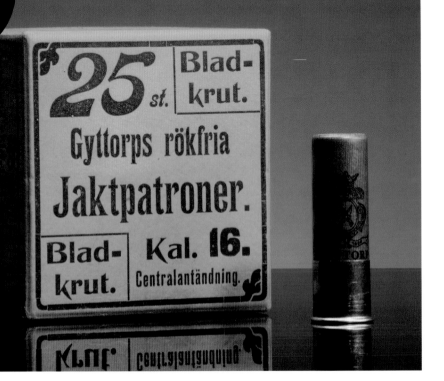

PROJECT
pucko
DESIGNER
peter neumeister
mattias lindstedt
tobias andersson
CLIENT
pucko

PROJECT
vitamin well
DESIGNER
peter neumeister
mattias lindstedt
tobias andersson
CLIENT
vitamin well

country
SWEDEN

CITY
bromma
STUDIO
sara strand

PROJECT
aomori apples
DESIGNER
sara strand
CLIENT
school project at broby grafiska

AOMORI APPLES FROM JAPAN
Åomori

PROJECT
children's tea
DESIGNER
sara strand
CLIENT
*personal project
at broby grafiska*

PROJECT
love fonts memo
DESIGNER
sara strand
CLIENT
*personal project
at broby grafiska*

PROJECT
fish, bird, dog and cat
DESIGNER
sara strand
CLIENT
*personal project
at broby grafiska*

country
SWEDEN

CITY **PROJECT**
stockholm *koberg*
STUDIO **DESIGNER**
designkontoret *ulf berlin*
Silver kb *cajsa bratt*
CLIENT
koberg vilt

PROJECT
ica cream
DESIGNER
ulf berlin
steven webb
roland persson
CLIENT
ica ab

PROJECT
ica crunchy
DESIGNER
ulf berlin
steven webb
roland persson
CLIENT
ica ab

ICA
apelsinjuice

INGREDIENSER
Apelsinjuice med fruktkött.
NÄRINGSVÄRDE/100 G
Energivärde .... 170 kJ / 40 kcal
Protein 0,1g
Kolhydrat 10g
Fett 0,1g
FÖRVARING
Kylvara. Förvaras i kylskåp (högst +8°C).
HÅLLBARHET
Bäst före: Se datummärkning.
FÖRPACKNING
Förpackningen sorteras som pappersförpackning och korken
som hårdplast.
INFORMATION
Producerad i Tyskland för ICA AB, 171 93 Solna, Sverige.
Kundkontakt (S): 020-83 33 33 eller www.ICA.se

ICA
apelsinjuice
från färska frukter
har en söt smak
av solmogna apelsiner
med fruktkött
1 LITER

ICA
apelsinjuice
från färska frukter
har en söt smak
av solmogna apelsiner
med fruktkött.
1 LITER

ICA
röd grapejuice

INGREDIENSER
Röd Grapefruktjuice med fruktkött.
NÄRINGSVÄRDE/100 G
Energivärde .... 140 kJ / 30 kcal
Protein 0,5g
Kolhydrat 7,5g
Fett 0,1g
FÖRVARING
Kylvara. Förvaras i kylskåp (högst +8°C).
HÅLLBARHET
Bäst före: Se datummärkning.
FÖRPACKNING
Förpackningen sorteras som pappersförpackning och korken
som hårdplast.
INFORMATION
Producerad i Tyskland för ICA AB, 171 93 Solna, Sverige.
Kundkontakt (S): 020-83 33 33 eller www.ICA.se

ICA
röd
grapejuice
från färska frukter
har en balanserad smak av
sötma och beska från röd grape
med fruktkött
1 LITER

ICA
röd
grapejuice
från färska frukter
har en balanserad smak av
sötma och beska från röd grape
med fruktkött
1 LITER

PROJECT
ica juice
DESIGNER
ulf berlin
linus östberg
roland persson
CLIENT
ica ab

PROJECT
ica rootcrisps
DESIGNER
ulf berlin
linus östberg
roland persson
CLIENT
ica ab

ICA

ROTFRUKTS CHIPS

KRISPIGA, KNAPRIGA SKIVOR AV

PALSTERNACKA

RÖDBETA

SÖTPOTATIS

& MOROT

SOLROSOLJA & HAVSSALT
ENDAST 0,8% SALT
100 GRAM

PROJECT
cliniderm pure & clean
DESIGNER
ulf berlin
eva aggerborg
CLIENT
aco skin nordic ab

PROJECT
ica baby diapers
DESIGNER
ulf berlin
cajsa bratt
roland persson
CLIENT
ica ab

SPOTLESS
TREATING
COVER STICK

▸ Conceals and
  dries out spots
▸ **No perfume**

ACO
APOTEKENS COMPOSITA

SPOTLESS
TWO-IN-ONE
BLEMISH TREATING
MOISTURISER

▸ Treats and prevents
  blackheads and spots
▸ Moisturises and smoothes
  the skin
▸ **No perfume**

ACO
APOTEKENS COMPOSITA

SPOTLESS
BLEMISH
TREATING

DAILY
PURIFYING TONER

▸ Cleanses pores
▸ Prevents blackheads
▸ **No perfume**

ACO
APOTEKENS COMPOSITA

SPOTLESS
DEEP
CLEANSING

DAILY
FACE WASH

▸ Gently cleanses pores
▸ Treats and prevents
  breakouts
▸ **With perfume**

ACO
APOTEKENS COMPOSITA

PROJECT
aco spotless
DESIGNER
andré hindersson
blanca wallner
monica holm
CLIENT
aco skin nordic ab

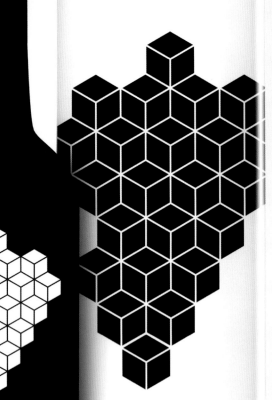

country
<u>SWEDEN</u>

CITY   **PROJECT**
karlskrona   *charles le chat*

STUDIO   **DESIGNER**
victor eide *victor eide*

CLIENT
student work

Charles le Chat

Shiraz   2004

Charles le Chat is a old wine with a modern apperence. The whole thing started back in 1747 when Sébastien Baudoin start produce wine on his wine yard on the plateau of Pomerol. The commune of Pomerol is found on the right bank of the Gironde Estuary in the Bordeaux region of Southwestern France. The Charles le Chat comes from the cat with the name Charles lived on the farm on the time Sébastien Baudoin start produce is wine, and ther for its named Charles le Chat

12,5 % 75cl

Charles le Chat

Shiraz
2004

country
SWEDEN

CITY   **PROJECT**
stockholm   staropramen
STUDIO   **DESIGNER**
werk   armin
             osmancevic
             CLIENT
             staropramen

PROJECT
carlsberg 900
DESIGNER
armin osmancevic
CLIENT
carlsberg

SWITZERLAND

47°00` NORTH / 8°00` EAST

CH

country
SWITZERLAND

CITY   **PROJECT**
sagogn   *fine food*
STUDIO   **DESIGNER**
remo   *remo caminada*
caminada   **CLIENT**
graphic   *andreas*
design   *caminada*
             schauenstein

Es war einmal ein Drache,
der konnte kein Feuer spucken,
sondern nur Tomatensauce.
Eines Tages wurde er von einem blondgelockten Ritter
in einer silbernen Rüstung er-
schlagen, und es stellte sich
heraus: in den Adern des
Drachens floss nur Ketchup.
War der Drache ein Betrüger?
Ein Spion aus Disney World,
Hollywood oder sonst einer
Traumfabrik?

Gion Mathias Cavelty

Peperoniconfit
Piment confit

Auberginenkaviar
Caviar d'aubergine

Tomatenessenz
Essence de tomates

Mandeltuille
Tuile d'amande

Schwarze Nüsse
Noix noires de Pécan

Quittenchutney
Chutney au coing

Apéro-Kürbiskerne
Graine de courge apér

Panforte

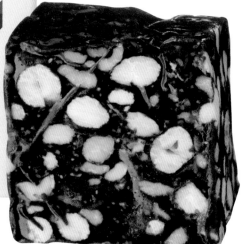

Schokococo-Tuille

Gemüseessenz
Essence de légumes

Kalb-Reduktion
Réduction de veau

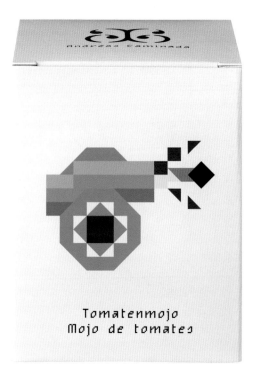

Tomatenmojo
Mojo de tomates

Apéro-Sonnenblumenker
Graine de tournesol apé

Zitronenconfit
Citron confit

PROJECT
cd project ''temps''
365 cds, each
represents one day
DESIGNER
remo caminada
CLIENT
gion andrea
casanova

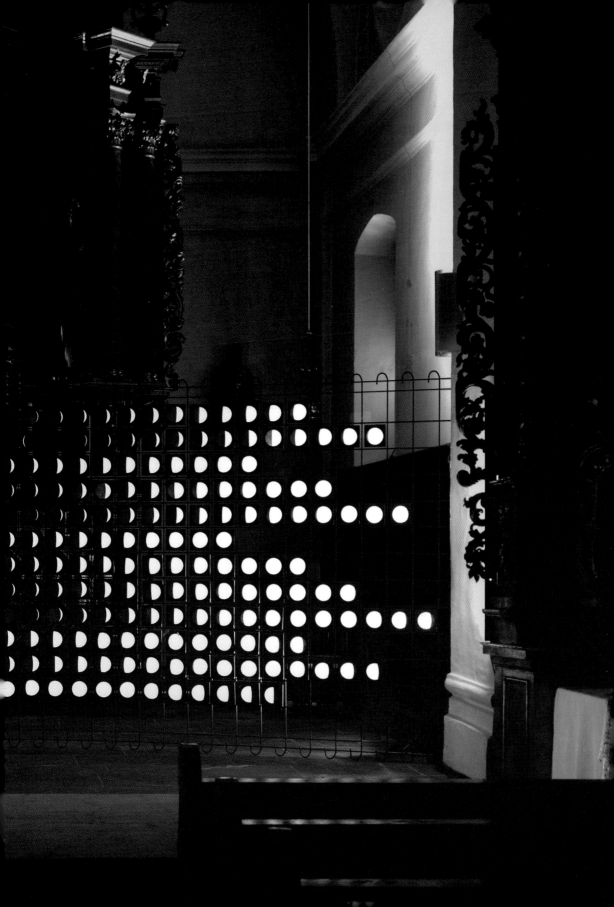

MIGROS Sélection | Culatello di Parma

MIGROS | Sélection | Salame al tartufo | Salami aux truffes
Salami mit Trüffeln
Salame al tartufo

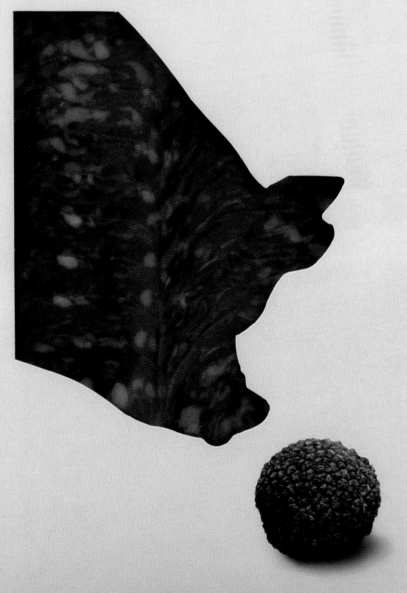

Serviervorschlag

MIGROS

Sélection
Carnaroli Risotto

MIGROS

Sélection
Riz Basmati

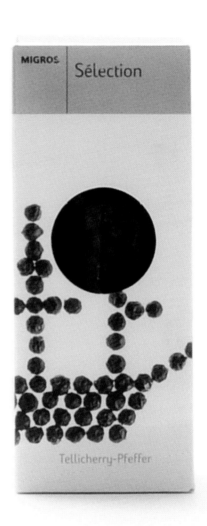

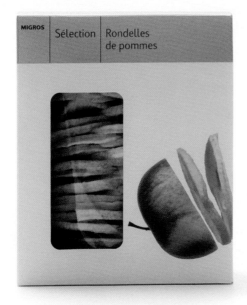

MIGROS | Sélection | Rondelles de pommes

MIGROS | Sélection

Purè di tartufi d'estate

MIGROS

Sélection
Blumenpfeffer

6 Schweizer Bio-Eier | Œufs bio suisses | Uova bio svizzere
Freilandhaltung | Elevage en plein air | Allevamento all'aperto

PROJECT
migros bio
STUDIO
schneiter meier külling
CLIENT
migros

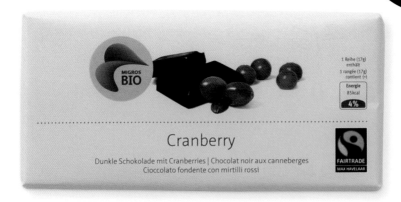

Cranberry

Dunkle Schokolade mit Cranberries | Chocolat noir aux canneberges
Cioccolato fondente con mirtilli rossi

Crémant

Zartbitterschokolade | Chocolat noir
Cioccolato amaro

Tomatensuppe
Soupe de tomate
Zuppa di pomodoro

400 ml

3.40

Würfelzucker
Sucre en morceaux
Zucchero in zollette

Rotweinessig
Vinaigre de vin rouge
Aceto di vino rosso

Himbeer
à la framboise
al lampone

500 ml

8-Korn Zopf
Tresse 8 céréales
Treccia 8 cereali

Brotfertigmischung
Mélange pour pâte à pain
Miscela già pronta per pane

Biotta

Preiselbeer Plus
Airelles rouges Plus
Mirtilli rossi Plus

Chnöpflimehl
Farine à Spätzli
Farina per Spätzli

1 kg

PROJECT
helvepharm
STUDIO
schneiter
meier
külling
CLIENT
helvepharm

Simvastatin
Helvepharm

Blutlipidsenker/
HMG-CoA-Reduktase-Hemm

40
98

Dexamethason
Helvepharm

Glucocorticoid-Therapie

5
25   mg/ml

Ampullen

Lisinopril
Helvepharm

Antihypertonikum

5
30   Tabletten

Amlodipin
Helvepharm

Calciumantagonist

5
100

Terbinaf
Helvepha

Antimykotikum

250
28

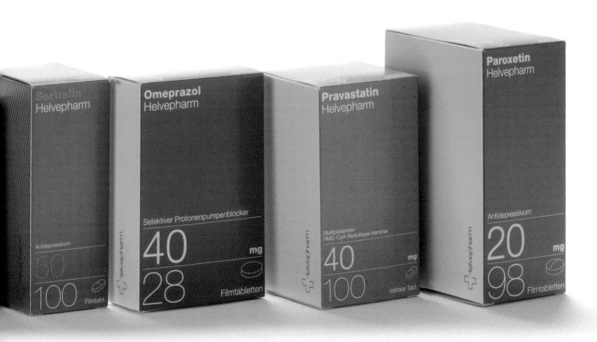

PROJECT
traktor
STUDIO
schneiter
meier
külling
CLIENT
traktor

PROJECT
globus organic
STUDIO
schneiter
meier
külling
CLIENT
globus

organic

Carnaroli-Reis superfino/
Riz Carnaroli extra-fin

organic

Viamala-Bergkäse/
Viamala-fromage de montagne

organic

Zitronenessig/
Vinaigre au citron

organic

Bohnenkaffee Machu Picchu/
Café en grains Machu Picchu

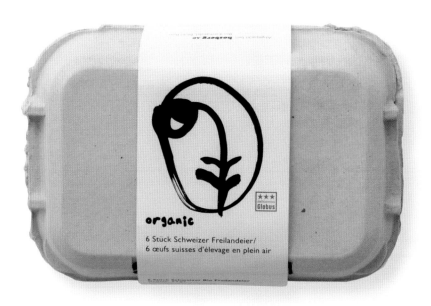

THE NETHERLANDS
52°30` NORTH / 5°45` EAST
NL

Ring Amsterdam

Amersfoort 44
Utrecht 42
Den Haag 65

 A 10 noord  A 10 noord

afrit [s 115]
Schellingwoude
Durgerdam

country
THE NETHERLANDS

CITY   PROJECT
haarlem   not a box
STUDIO   DESIGNER
studio   david graas
david   CLIENT
graas   self initiated

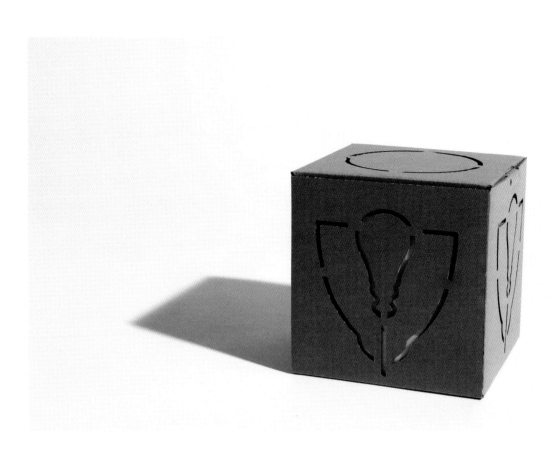

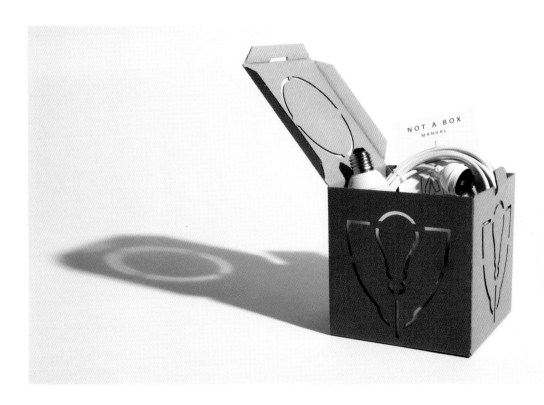

PROJECT
fiy junior
DESIGNER
david graas
CLIENT
self initiated

country
THE NETHERLANDS

CITY   PROJECT
amsterdam   hema
STUDIO   DESIGNER
koeweiden   koeweiden
postma   postma
CLIENT
hema

HEMA
Melkchocolade met
hazelnoot
Chocolat au lait aux
noisettes
Milch-Haselnuss-
Schokolade

HEMA
Koggetjes
Roomboter - Pur beurre - Butter

HEMA
Mini cake naturel
Mini cake nature
Mini-Sandkuchen
Roomboter - Pur beurre - Butter

HEMA
Fijne wafels
Gaufrettes fines
Feine Waffeln
Roomboter - Pur beurre - Butter

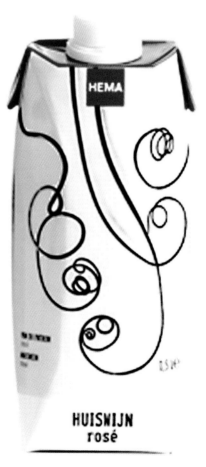

HUISWIJN
wit droog

HUISWIJN
rosé

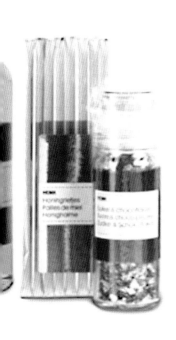

country
THE NETHERLANDS

CITY   **PROJECT**
amsterdam   *bolletje wol*
STUDIO   *packaging*
studio   **DESIGNER**
kluif   *paul roeters*
sander tiden
CLIENT
bolletje

PROJECT
packaging crafts
products "art&fun"
DESIGNER
paul roeters
anne van arkel
CLIENT
hema

FAIR TRADE HATS
MADE IN NEPAL

BOLLETJE *wol*

THIS UNIQUE HAT WAS
HANDMADE IN NEPAL BY
Shahana Rita Indria

IT WAS MADE UNDER THE STRICT REGULATIONS OF FAIR
TRADE. THIS IS WHY YOU GET A UNIQUE, HANDCRAFTED HAT
AND THEY GET THE MONEY THEY DESERVE.

ART&FUN

Popje maken
Création de Poupées
Puppe basteln

Compleet met alle benodigdheden
Avec tout le nécessaire
Komplett mit Zubehör

HEMA

ART&FUN

Pompon figuren maken
Création de personnages avec pompons
Bommel-Figuren basteln

Compleet met alle benodigdheden
Avec tout le nécessaire
Komplett mit Zubehören

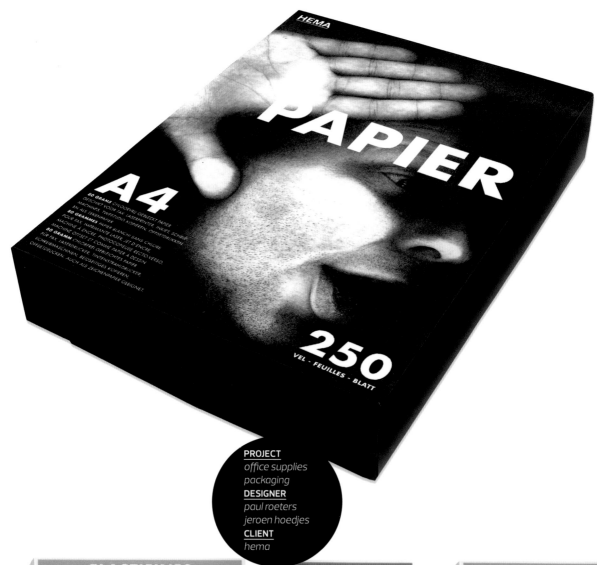

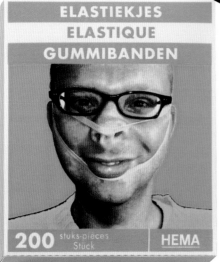

PROJECT
office supplies
packaging
DESIGNER
paul roeters
jeroen hoedjes
CLIENT
hema

PROJECT
presskit "zippy"
DESIGNER
paul roeters
helen bucher
CLIENT
hema

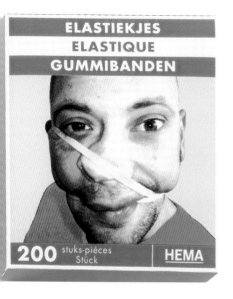

PROJECT
markers&pencils
packaging
DESIGNER
paul roeters
anne van arkel
CLIENT
hema

HEMA

ART&FUN

Kleurpotloden
Crayons de couleu
Farbstifte

Lindehout • glutenvrij
Bois de Tilleul • sans gluten
Lindenholz • Glutenfrei

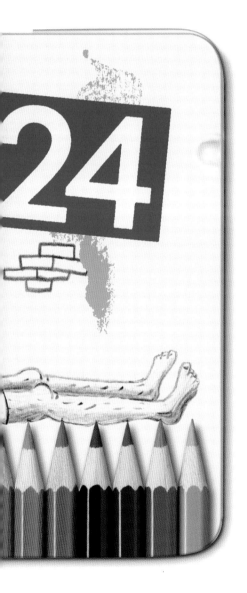

UNITED KINGDOM

54°00` NORTH / 21°00` EAST

UK

country
UNITED KINGDOM

CITY | PROJECT
southsea | choice cuts
STUDIO | DESIGNER
ilovedust | ilovedust
| CLIENT
| choice cuts

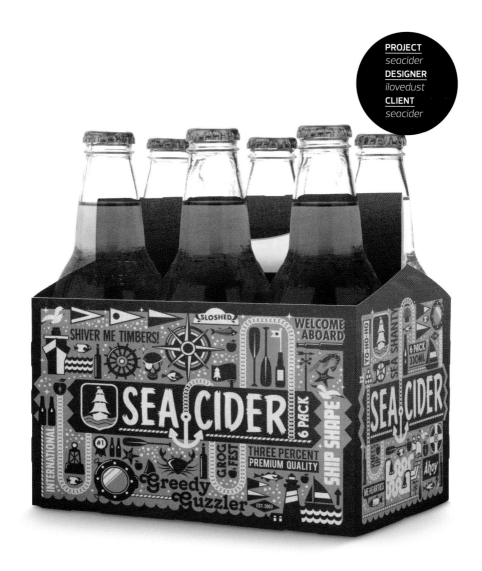

PROJECT
seacider
DESIGNER
ilovedust
CLIENT
seacider

PROJECT
bill's milkshakes
DESIGNER
ilovedust
CLIENT
bill's milkshakes

country
UNITED KINGDOM

CITY   **PROJECT**
leeds   *ambrosia custard*
STUDIO   *brand idendity &*
joe stephenson   *packaging*
graphic design   **DESIGNER**
   joe stephenson
CLIENT
ambrosia

PROJECT
bassetts allsorts
brand idendity &
packaging
DESIGNER
joe stephenson
CLIENT
bassetts

Fedrigoni's GELATERIA

Come and cool off from the
summer heat with a refreshing
scoop of Fedrigoni's traditional
Italian gelato ice cream!

A place for ice cream!
Thursday 8th July, 2010
7:00—10:30pm

Fedrigoni London Showroom
5th floor, Diamond House
36–38 Hatton Garden
London EC1N 8EB

RSVP online at
fedrigoni.co.uk/gelateria

FEDRIGONI

PROJECT
*fedrigoni's gelateria
event idendity&
packaging*
DESIGNER
joe stephenson
CLIENT
*fedrigoni paper
merchants*

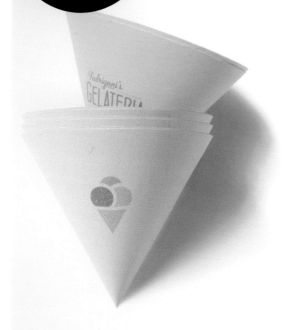

PROJECT
common ground
coffee house
brand idendity&packaging
DESIGNER
joe stephenson
CLIENT
common ground
coffee house

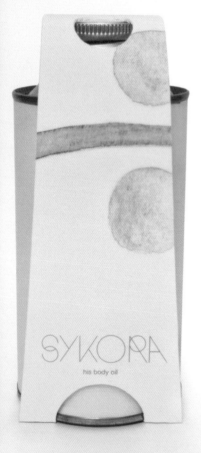
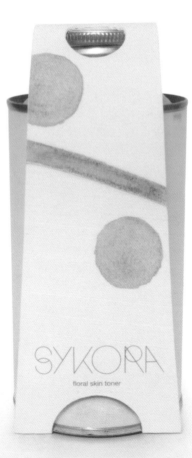

PROJECT
*sykora organic
cosmetics
brand idendity&
packaging*
DESIGNER
joe stephenson
CLIENT
*sykora organic
cosmetics*

country
UNITED KINGDOM

CITY **PROJECT**
london *prism eyewear*
STUDIO *case*
sabotage pkg **DESIGNER**
sabotage pkg
CLIENT
prism
eyewear

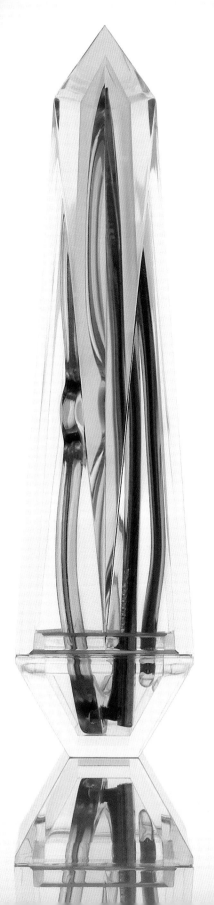

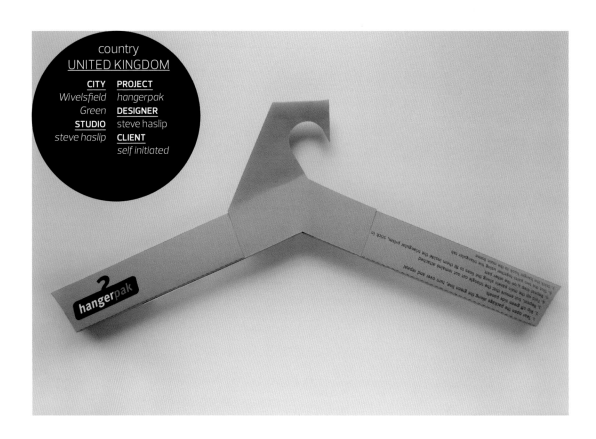

country
UNITED KINGDOM

CITY | **PROJECT**
Wivelsfield | *hangerpak*
Green | **DESIGNER**
STUDIO | steve haslip
steve haslip | **CLIENT**
| *self initiated*

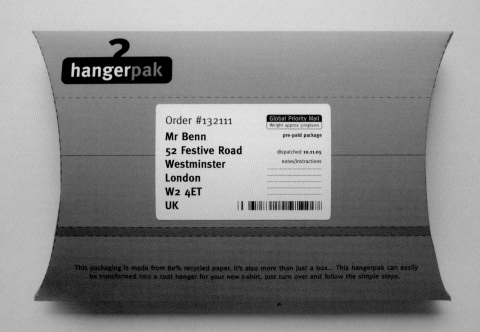

Order #132111

Mr Benn
52 Festive Road
Westminster
London
W2 4ET
UK

Global Priority Mail
Weight approx 300grams

pre-paid package

dispatched 10.11.05

notes/instructions
....
....
....
....

This packaging is made from 80% recycled paper. It's also more than just a box... This hangerpak can easily be transformed into a coat hanger for your new t-shirt. Just turn over and follow the simple steps.

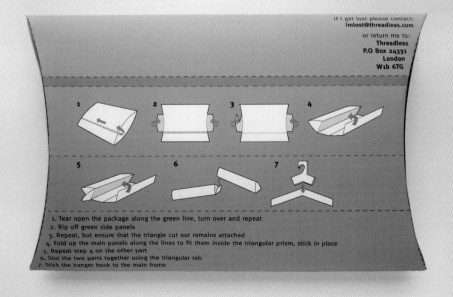

1. Tear open the package along the green line, turn over and repeat
2. Rip off green side panels
3. Repeat, but ensure that the triangle cut out remains attached
4. Fold up the main panels along the lines to fit them inside the triangular prism, stick in place
5. Repeat step 4 on the other part
6. Slot the two parts together using the triangular tab
7. Stick the hanger hook to the main frame

country
UNITED KINGDOM

CITY   PROJECT
derby   homebase
STUDIO   seed packaging
vicky barlow DESIGNER
            vicky barlow
            CLIENT
            student work

CARROTS

To be planted
13mm into
the ground

Can grow
up to one
foot deep

H MEBASE **GROW YOUR OWN**

308

309

ROMANIA

44°27'N / 26°10'E

RO

RUSSIA

55°45'N / 37°35'E

RU

SERBIA

44°49'N / 20°28'E

SLOVAKIA

48°40'N / 19°30'E

SK

UKRAINE

50°24'N / 30°34'E

UA

TURKEY

39°57'N / 32°54'E

TR

country
CZECH REPUBLIC

CITY
prague
STUDIO
stas sipovic
design

PROJECT
zürcher
identity concept
DESIGNER
stas sipovic
CLIENT
zürcher

Zürcher

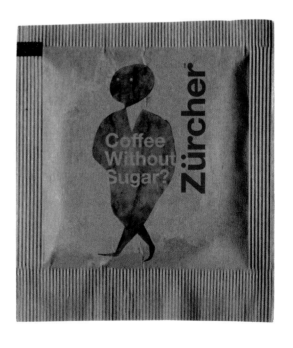

1. Я ВСТРЕТИЛ СОЛНЦЕ   3:23
2. ОСТАТЬСЯ РАССТАТЬСЯ   3:38
3. Я ПОТЕРЯЛ   4:06
4. ПАДЕНИЕ ВВЕРХ   3:48
5. СНЫ   3:59
6. ТУДА ГДЕ НЕБО   3:41
7. СТО ЛЕТ ТИШИНЫ   3:18
8. ОБЫЧНАЯ ЖИЗНЬ   3:47
9. ПРОСТО ЛЮБОВЬ   3:25
10. ПЕРВЫЙ ДЕНЬ МИРА   3:57

© А.А. Романушкин, О.В. Черников, 2009

PROJECT
access level
cd packaging
DESIGNER
stas sipovic
CLIENT
access level
music band

УРОВЕНЬ ДОСТУПА:
Олег Черников
Андрей Романушкин
Николай Скворцов

myspace.com/accesslevel

country
ROMANIA

CITY   PROJECT
lasi   magni
STUDIO   DESIGNER
andrei d. popa   andrei d. popa
         CLIENT
         magni

MAGNI
chocolate & honey
100g e

MAGNI
chocolate & milk
100g e

MAGNI
white chocolate & honey
100g e

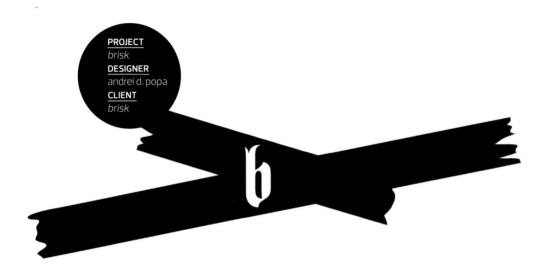

PROJECT
brisk
DESIGNER
andrei d. popa
CLIENT
brisk

country
RUSSIA

CITY | **PROJECT**
novosibirsk | crestmilk
STUDIO | **DESIGNER**
hattomonkey | aleksey kurchin
 | **CLIENT**
 | milk collection

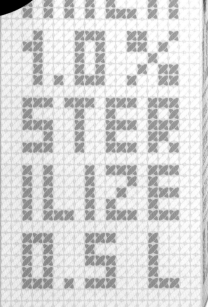
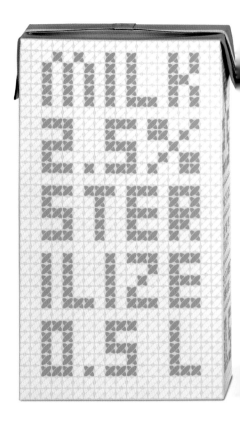

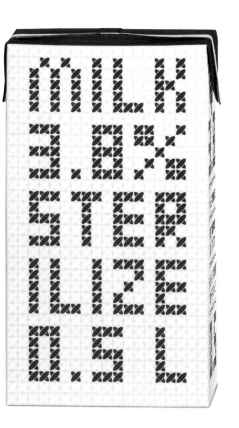

PROJECT
cowmilk
DESIGNER
aleksey kurchin
CLIENT
nmk

PROJECT
molokoshka
DESIGNER
aleksey kurchin
CLIENT
nmk

PROJECT
niagara
DESIGNER
aleksey kurchin
CLIENT
niagara

Milk cocktail
by Joe
Strawberry

Wheat Flour, Vegetable Oil(Palm Oil, Rapeseed, Soy and Corn Oil), Sugar, Lactose, Whole Milk Powder, Shortening, Butter, Salt, Dried Strawberry, Skim Milk Powder, Dextrin, Artificial Flavor(Strawberry and Milk), Red Beet Color, Soy Lecithin, Trisodium, Phosphate, Sodium Bicarbonate, Contains Milk, Wheat, and Soy

300 ml

PROJECT
milk cocktails
by joe
DESIGNER
aleksey kurchin
CLIENT
milk collection

PROJECT
toothpaste noon
DESIGNER
aleksey kurchin
CLIENT
noon

PROJECT
hot sauces and spices hashi
DESIGNER
aleksey kurchin
CLIENT
interra

country
RUSSIA

CITY   **PROJECT**
moscow   *sexy tina*
STUDIO   *35% milky liquor*
truerender.ru   **DESIGNER**
pavel gubin
CLIENT
self initiated

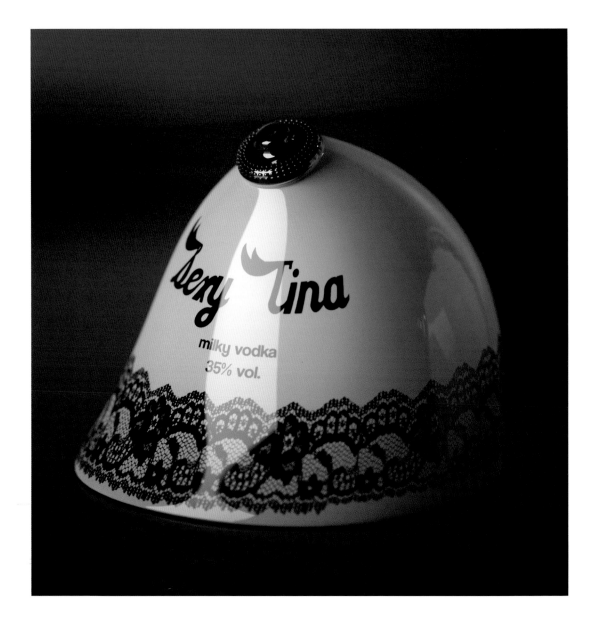

country
SERBIA

CITY
belgrade
STUDIO
coba&
associates

PROJECT
adore chocolat
DESIGNER
slobodan
jovanovic´
jana orsolic´
CLIENT
adore

PROJECT
selection rakia
DESIGNER
coba&associates
CLIENT
rakia bar

СЕЛЕКЦИЈА®

DOMAĆA RAKIJA
IZ MALIH PODRUMA SRBIJE

DOMAĆA RAKIJA | DUNJEVAČA
Nº 1 | PODRUM GOLOMEJA
DOUBLE DISTILLED QUINCE BRANDY

World famous
·PRODUCT OF SERBIA·

RAKIA BAR
SINCE 2006

СЕЛЕКЦИЈА

DOMAĆA RAKIJA
IZ MALIH PODRUMA SRBIJE

DOMAĆA RAKIJA | DUNJEVAČA
Nº 1 | PODRUM GOLOMEJA
DOUBLE DISTILLED QUINCE BRANDY

World famous
·PRODUCT OF SERBIA·

RAKIA BAR
ORIGINAL

country
<u>SLOVAKIA</u>

CITY **PROJECT**
trnava *tatratea*
STUDIO **DESIGNER**
pergamen *pergamen*
slovakia *slovakia*
CLIENT
karloff

52‰

TATRATEA

STRONG
ORIGINAL
FROM
THE HEART
OF THE TATRA
MOUNTAINS

PROJECT
terra parna
DESIGNER
pergamen
slovakia
CLIENT
zenagro

SVÄTOVAVRINECKÉ

Jemné tmavorubinové víno zrejúce
v barikových sudoch so spektrom
vôní vanilky a kôstkového ovocia.

TERRA PARNA

2008

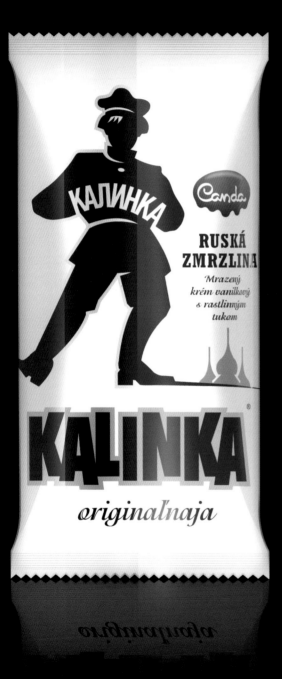

PROJECT
kalinka ice cream
DESIGNER
pergamen slovakia
CLIENT
canda

PROJECT
karloff brandy
special
DESIGNER
pergamen
slovakia
CLIENT
karloff

PROJECT
pierre baguette
DESIGNER
pergamen
slovakia
CLIENT
fekollini

country
<u>TURKEY</u>

<u>CITY</u>   <u>PROJECT</u>
istanbul   salt&pepper cell
<u>STUDIO</u>   <u>DESIGNER</u>
antrepo   mehmet
design   gozetlik
industry   <u>CLIENT</u>
    antrepo
    shop.com

country
UKRAINE

CITY
istanbul
STUDIO
reynolds and reyner

PROJECT
antismoke pack
DESIGNER
alexander andrews artemy kulique
CLIENT
self initiated

PROJECT
colier
DESIGNER
alexander andrews
artemy kulique
CLIENT
self initiated

INDEX STUDIOS

Studio: Neumeister
gic Design AB
Contact person: Peter
Neumeister
City: Stockholm
Web: www.neumeister.se

Studio: Sara Strand
Contact person: Sara
Strand
City: Bromma
Web: www.sarastrand.se

Studio: Designkontoret
Silver KB
Contact person: Maja Wet-
terberg,
City: Stockholm
Web: silver.se

Studio: Victor Eide
Contact person: Victor Eide
City: Karlskrona
Web: www.victoreide.com

Studio: WERK
Contact person: Armin
Osmancevic
City: Stockholm
Web: www.werk.se

SWITZERLAND

Studio: Remo Caminada,
graphic design
Contact person: Remo
Caminada
City: Sagogn
Web: www.remocaminada.
com

Studio: Schneiter Meier
Külling
City: Zürich
Web: www.smek.ch

THE NETHERLANDS

Studio: Studio David Graas
Contact person: David
Graas
City: Haarlem
Web: www.davidgraas.com

Studio: Koeweiden Postma
City: Amsterdam
Web: www.koeweiden-
postma.com

Studio: Studio Kluif
City: Amsterdam
Web: www.studiokluif.nl

UNITED KINGDOM

Studio: ilovedust
City: Southsea
Web: www.ilovedust.com

Studio: Joe Stephenson
Graphic Design
Contact person: Joe Ste-
phenson
City: Leeds
Web: www.joestephenson.
co.uk

Studio: Sabotage PKG
City: London
Web: www.sabotagepkg.
com

Studio: Steve Haslip
Contact person: Steve
Haslip
City: Brooklyn New York /
London
Web: www.stevehaslip.com

Studio: Vicky Barlow
Contact person: Vicky
Barlow
City: Derby
Web: www.vickybarlow.
co.uk

THE BEST OF THE EAST

CZECH REPUBLIC

Studio: Stas Sipovic Design
Contact person: Stas
Sipovic
City: Prague
Web: www.stassipovic.com

ROMANIA

Studio: Andrei Popa
Contact person: Andrei D.
Popa
City: Lasi
Website: www.andreipopa.
com

RUSSIA

Studio: Hattomonkey
Contact person: Aleksey
Kurchin
City: Novosibirsk
Website: www.hattomon-
key.ru

Studio: True Dot / True
render
Contact person: Duitry
Kuznetsoy
City: Moscow
Website: truedot.ru

Associates
son: Jane

lgrade
Website: www.coba.rs

SLOVAKIA

Studio: PERGAMEN
City: Trnava
Web: www.pergamen.sk

TURKEY

Studio: Antrepo Design
Industry
Contact person: Mehmet
Gözetlik
City: Istanbul
Web: www.antrepo4.com

UKRAINE

Studio: Reynolds and
Reyner
Contact person: Artemy
Kulique
City: Kiev
Web: www.reynoldsan-
dreyner.com

LIFTPLAA